Second Grade Homeschooling

(Includes Social Science, Math and Science)

By Thomas Bell, Greg Sherman, and Terri Raymond

Home School Brew Press

www.HomeSchoolBrew.com

Table of Contents

Disclaimer

This book was developed for parents and students of no particular state; while it is based on common core standards, it is always best to check with your state board to see what will be included on testing.

About Us

Homeschool Brew was started for one simple reason: to make affordable Homeschooling books! When we began looking into homeschooling our own children, we were astonished at the cost of curriculum. Nobody ever said homeschool was easy, but we didn't know that the cost to get materials would leave us broke.

We began partnering with educators and parents to start producing the same kind of quality content that you expect in expensive books...but at a price anyone can afford.

We are still in our infancy stages, but we will be adding more books every month. We value your feedback, so if you have any comments about what you like or how we can do better, then please let us know!

To add your name to our mailing list, go here: http://www.homeschoolbrew.com/mailing-list.html

Second Grade Science
For Homeschool or Extra Practice

By Thomas Bell

Physical Science #1: Measuring Objects

Objects can be described based on physical characteristics like size, shape, color, or texture. These are very simple forms of measurement. Objects can be grouped together or separated based on certain characteristics as well. In science, objects can be measured using tools like a ruler or a scale to provide more detail on the properties of the object. For example, a rock can be described using words (or qualitatively) as being smooth, gray, circular, and flat. To be specific, you could weigh the rock on a scale to know its mass, or measure the length of the rock using a ruler. In this section, you will explore more about measurements, the different types of measurement or data that can be recorded and simple science instruments that can be used to measure objects.

Types of Scientific Data

There are two main categories of scientific data: qualitative and quantitative.

If you refer to the word *quality*, this will help you remember what qualitative data is. Qualitative data is based on using words, or your five senses (sight, taste, hearing, touch, and smell) to describe an object. Take the animals below, for example, you could describe these animals qualitatively.

What could you say about these animals, using just words to describe the animals' size (big versus small), shape, fur/skin color, fur/skin texture, living environment, method of movement, etc. You might qualitatively describe the animals using some of the statements below:

- The dog is bigger than the hamster
- The frogs are yellow and blue and have slimy skin
- The snake is green, thin, and long
- The rabbit is tan, with large ears, and a soft fur coat

- The parrot has green and yellow feathers, but the other bird is smaller and has orange feathers

The key to qualitative data is that it is what can be observed with your five senses. This type of data does not use numbers or units of measurement like ounces, pounds, meters, inches, or liters.

Quantitative data, on the other hand, refers to the word *quantity*, or the number or amount of something. This type of data involves using numbers and units of measurement to describe the characteristics of objects. You may use statements like, "there are 5 more blue flowers than red flowers", or "the bowling ball weighs 3 pounds". Quantitative data is very important in science and there are several different scientific tools that can be used to measure objects and get detailed information about the quantity or amount related to an object. What types of quantitative statements could you make based on the animals picture on the previous page?

You might quantitatively describe the animals using some of the statements below:

- There are 2 frogs, 1 snake, and 1 rabbit
- The rabbit weighs 5 pounds
- The dog, the hamster, and the cat all have 4 legs
- The fish live in a bowl with 20 cups of water
- The snake is 3 feet long from head to tail

Now that we have discussed the types of data that can be collected, let's look at the types of quantitative measurements that calculated in science.

Units of Measurement

Length

Length can refer to the height or the width of an object. How long is it? In science, scientists generally measure length in meters, using a meter stick. However, in the United States, we often use inches or feet to measure the length of objects. A table may be 48 inches (4 feet) long, or your height may be 60 inches (5 feet). Length can also be described as distance or the length of travel from start to finish. We often travel long distances that to use inches or feet would be a very large number. Larger units for length like yards or miles can be used. The scientific unit for distance is the kilometer, however, we often use miles to describe distance. A marathon is 26.2 miles, whereas a football field is approximately 120 yards (which is equal to 360 feet). Understanding what you are trying to measure will help you determine the appropriate unit of measurement to use. Let's look at a few images and discuss the unit of measurement for length that would be best.

What units should be used to measure the car? You could probably use inches, but that would be a lot of counting. Instead, you would measure the car in feet. How about the cellphone? This is a smaller object in comparison to the car, so inches would work just fine for this object. Let's know look at weight.

Weight

Weight can be measured in several different units. Scientists use grams or kilograms to measure the weight of objects. In the United States, pounds or ounces are used to describe the weight of objects. For example, when you were born, you may have weighed 8 pounds and 4 ounces. The pounds and ounces help to define your weight. If you were to measure an ant, you would have to use a much smaller unit for weight. A single ant would not weigh a pound or anything near that amount, but we could measure an ant in a smaller unit called a gram. A gram is 0.002 pounds, or you could say that 1 pound is 454 grams. That's a lot of grams for one pound! An ant may weigh 0.001 grams, which is a very small number. For very large objects, like an elephant, pounds are too small of a unit for weight. You could use pounds, but the weight of an elephant in pounds is approximately 15,000 pounds. That's a lot of pounds! Instead, you might use tons for the unit of measurement. One ton is equal to 2,000 pounds. The weight of an adult male elephant is approximately 7.5 tons! Look at the images below and try to predict what unit of measurement would be best to measure the weight of the object.

What weight unit would be the best for the rocking chair? The rocking chair is not extremely small, so grams would not be the best unit. The rocking chair is not as large as the truck and could be lifted by an adult. So, using pounds may be okay for the rocking chair. What about the truck? This is a large object that is not easily lifted, so tons would be the better unit for its weight. Let's now look at how we measure liquids.

Volume

We can use even more units of measurements to measure the volume (or amount) of a liquid. What units of measurement have you heard of in relationship to liquids? We may buy a *gallon* of milk, or a recipe may call for a *cup* of milk, or a tomato sauce can may have 64 *ounces* of tomatoes, and even still you may buy a 2 *liter* bottle of soda. Like with the other units of measurements, the one you use depends on the amount and size of the liquid you are trying to measure. Scientists generally use liters for volume, however, in the United States, we often use liters, cups, or ounces. What volume unit would be best for the images below?

Other Units of Measurement

We may measure other things like: time and temperature. Time can be measured in years, months, weeks, days, hours, minutes, or seconds. Temperature can be measured in Fahrenheit (in the United States) or in degrees Celsius. The weather report is a great example of how temperature is measured. The meteorologist may comment that, "today's high temperature will be 75°F".

Tools for Measurement

Now that we have discussed the types of measurements and the units of measurement, let's look at the scientific tools or instruments that can be used to determine these measurements.

For length, we can use a simple ruler, a meter stick, a yard stick, or even measuring tape. Depending on the distance or length you are trying to measure will determine which of these instruments is best to use.

For weight, we often use a scale or balance. This can be seen in the doctor's office which records your weight or in the grocery store when your parents weigh the fruit before they buy it. Some scales are extremely sensitive and are able to record very, very small weights, like the weight of an ant. Whereas other scales are very large and able to record large weights like tons.

For volume, you can use a beaker or graduated cylinder similar to the images below. Measuring cups or measuring spoons can also be used, especially when measuring volumes or amounts for recipes.

For time you may use a calendar, a clock, or even a stopwatch. Depending on the amount of time you are trying to measure will determine if a calendar (for longer periods of time) is better to use than a stopwatch (for shorter periods of time).

For temperature, we use thermometers. These can be in degrees Celsius or Fahrenheit. Some thermometers have both units, with Celsius on one side, and Fahrenheit on the other.

Classifying objects using qualitative and quantitative data is an important part of science. As you can see, there are lots of measurements we can take and even more types of scientific tools we can use to calculate those measurements.

Activities

#1 - Sliding is fun!

Note: For this experiment, you will want to have at least 3 people.

Materials:

- Flat surface with an edge, like a table or desk
- Deck of cards
- Paper
- Pencil
- Ruler

Procedure:

1. Divide the deck of cards evenly among the number of people that are present. For example, if there are 4 people, then each person will get 13 cards.

2. Place the card on the flat surface. One at a time, have each person place one finger on the card and flick or slide it forward toward the edge of the flat surface. The goal of this step is to slide the card far enough that it is as close as possible to the edge of the flat surface as possible.

3. Use a ruler to measure the length of the distance between the cards and the edge of the table/desk. You can use millimeters, centimeters, or inches, but it is important to use the same measurement each time.

4. Have each person go one at a time, repeating steps 2 and 3. Who slid their card the farthest?

What's happening?

Usually sliding cards across a table does not seem like a learning activity, but when math and measurement are involved, it can be! In this experiment you were able to practice measuring lengths and using a ruler.

#2– Jump, Jump, Jump Around

Note: For this experiment, you will need a partner.

Materials:

- One liquid crystal thermometer

- Stopwatch, or a watch that shows seconds

- Paper

- Pencil

Procedure:

1. Write a two-column chart; one column should state "resting" and the other should state "after exercise."

2. Have one person first sit down and hold a thermometer to their foreheads for approximately one minute.

3. After the minute is over, look at the temperature and record it on the paper.

4. Have the person get up and run in place or do jumping jacks for two minutes without resting.

5. When the two minutes are up, take their temperatures again. Write this number down on the paper.

6. Subtract the resting temperature from the after-exercise temperature. The remaining difference is how many degrees higher your temperature rose after exercising.

What's happening?

When you exercise, you probably feel hotter and begin to sweat. This experiment shows that you feel hotter and sweat because your temperature actually does rise when you exercise. We can determine the change in temperatures by subtracting the two temperatures.

#3: Who needs a ruler?

Materials:

- Metal paper clips (at least 50 of them)

- Paper and pencil

- Household objects (spoons, shoes, socks, tie, etc)

Procedure:

1. Find several objects around your house. Some should be short and some should be long.

2. Estimate how many paper clips will be needed to measure the object.

3. Line the paper clips one by one along the object and see how many paper clips are needed to measure it Was your estimate close?

4. You can link the paper clips together to create a paper clip measuring tool.

What's happening?

Other objects besides a ruler can be used to measure items. It is always good practice to make estimates and then use tools to test if your estimates were accurate. In this activity, you were able to explore with measuring items with paper clips. A paper clip is about an inch long, so really, you made your own flexible, growing ruler!

#4: The Mystery Box

Note: This activity works best with two people. One person should know what the object is, while the other person has to guess.

Materials:

- Shoebox with lid

- Small object (this should be able to fit in the showbox)

- Duct or MaskingTape (optional)

Procedure:

1. Place the object in the box.

2. Put the lid on the box. You may choose to tap it closed, if needed.

3. Give the closed box to the other person and ask them to figure out what is in the box. They cannot open the box, but they can shake the box.

Be sure to listen to the object in the box as it is shaken. Does it sound like it rolls? Is it heavy? Does it move around a lot in the box?

4.) After 5 minutes reveal what is in the box.

What's happening?

Since you cannot see the object in the box, you have to use your senses and make qualitative observations of the object. Based on how it sounded as it moved in the box, helps you determine certain characteristics of the object. It's not easy to figure out what the object is without knowing what it looks like, but with this activity you explored tapping into your other senses to help you solve the mystery.

#5: You're How Old?

Note: This is best done with at least two people.

Materials:

- Tree

- Flexible measuring tape

Procedure:

1. Find a tree.

2. Wrap the measuring tape around the trunk of the tree. Be sure you choose the widest part of the tree to measure.

3. Read the measurement in inches.

4. The number of inches is equal to the age of the tree. For example, a tree that is 40 inches around would be 40 years old!

What's happening?

Trees are a type of plant. Each year they grow a new layer of bark to protect themselves, growing about an inch wider every year. For a tree that has been cut down, you can count the rings on the tree stump from the center to the outer edge and this will also tell you the age of the tree. A tree makes a new ring every year when it grows a new layer of bark.

Quiz

Check Your Understanding

1.) What are the two types of scientific data?

2.) _____ data involves observations.

3.) _____ data involves numbers.

4.) True or False. Qualitative data involves your five senses.

5.) True or False. A ruler can be used to measure the volume of a liquid.

6.) Name three scientific instruments that can be used to measure length or distance.

7.) A football field should be measured with a _____.

8.) Name a unit for distance.

9.) Name a unit for weight.

10.) True or False. A beaker can be used to weigh an object.

11.) What weight unit is used for very tiny objects that have small weights?

12.) An elephant is best measured using _____.

13.) 2,000 pounds is equal to _____.

14.) Name three units of measurement for volume.

15.) Scientists use _____ to measure volume.

16.) Name one scientific instrument that can be used to measure the volume of a liquid.

17.) _____ and Fahrenheit are the two units used for measuring temperature.

18.) What scientific instrument is used to calculate the outside temperature?

19.) _____ can be used to measure time like how long it takes to run around the track.

20.) True or False. A calendar can be used to measure long periods of time.

Quiz Answers

1.) The two types of scientific data is qualitative and quantitative.
2.) Qualitative data involves observations.
3.) Quantitative data involves numbers.
4.) True. Qualitative data involves your five senses. These are observation statements that do not involve calculations or numbers.
5.) False. A ruler can be used to measure distances, especially short distances.
6.) The ruler, the meter stick, and the yard stick can all be used to measure length or distance.
7.) A football field should be measured with a yard stick. You could measure it with a ruler, it would just take a lot longer.
8.) The meter is a unit for distance. Other answers can include: inches, feet, miles, and/or kilometer.
9.) The pound is a unit for weigh. Other answers can include: grams, kilograms, tons, and/or ounces.
10.) False. A scale can be used to weigh an object. A beaker is used to determine the volume of a liquid.
11.) The gram is used for very tiny objects that have small weights like an ant.
12.) An elephant is best measured using tons. Remember tons are very large weight units for objects that are not easily picked up.
13.) 2,000 pounds is equal to one ton.
14.) Liter, ounces, cup are units of measurement for volume.
15.) Scientists use liters to measure volume.
16.) A beaker or a graduated cylinder can be used to measure the volume of a liquid.
17.) Celsius and Fahrenheit are the two units used for measuring temperature.
18.) A thermometer is used to calculate the outside temperature.
19.) A clock or stopwatch can be used to measure time like how long it takes to run around the track.
20.) True. A calendar can be used to measure long periods of time. This is true if you are measuring the number of days between Christmas and the 4th of July.

Physical Science #2: Motion and Magnets

Motion is all around us and is an important part of physics, a type of science. Some objects may move a lot, while others may not seem to move at all. Take Earth for example, if we are standing still, Earth is actually moving in an orbit around the Sun. Scientists have discovered ways to explain what movement or motion is and how motion can change.

Objects move based on force. In order for an object to move, some type of force has to act on the object to get it to move. For example, a cup will not fly off the table or move without you either picking up the cup or pushing it over. Your hand acts as the force, causing a motion to occur on the cup. Motion can be further described in terms of how fast the motion is. Velocity and speed are terms used by physicists to describe the rate or how quickly, or slowly an object is moving.

What is acceleration? How is that related to motion? Acceleration is how the velocity of an object changes over time. For example, if you are going on vacation and traveling on the highway at a speed of 65 miles per hour, that is your velocity. Note: this means that each hour, you cover a distance of 65 miles. Let's say that your parents are driving and they are able to keep that speed for 2 hours, until they notice a traffic jam ahead. They will likely have to slow down, say to 45 miles per hour. This changes your motion or your velocity. After 1 hour, once you pass the traffic jam, your parents may be able to increase their velocity to 65 miles per hour again. In this example, the velocity decreased, then increased. By knowing how the velocity changed and how long it changed for, you would be able to determine the car's acceleration. If we accelerate in a car that means the velocity is changing and it is increasing. If instead, we decelerate, that means the car is slowing down, so the velocity is changing, but this time it is decreasing.

The mass of an object can influence the motion of the object and the force needed to move the object. Think of it this way...

Is it easier to move a house or a toy block? A house has a large mass or weight and it can move, but you would need a large amount of force to push or pull the house. A toy block is small and has a small mass. This could easily be moved by you pushing it or picking it up.

There are types of motion. Motion can be simple or complex.

Simple motion movements are in a straight line. The object can be slowing down or speeding up, but its motion can be traced or tracked on a straight path. The movement of a bowling ball rolling down a bowling lane would be an example of simple movement.

Complex movements involve direction changes, like when an object is going in a circle, in a random path, or at an angle. When a baseball is hit in the air, its movement would be complex, as the ball travels up, at an angle, and then comes down to the ground.

Laws of Motion

Sir Isaac Newton, an English scientist put forth three principles or laws that applied to motion. These laws are used in physics to describe the movement of objects and how they behave as they move.

Newton's First Law of Motion: An object at rest will stay at rest and an object in motion will stay in motion, unless acted upon by an outside force. Take the bowling ball for example. If you were to place the ball down gently at the beginning of the lane, the ball is not likely to move and travel toward the pin. This is what Newton describes as "an object at rest, will stay at rest", meaning if the object is not moving, it will continue to not move. If we want the bowling ball to travel toward the bowling pins, then we would need to apply a force to move the ball. The force in this example can be your hands pushing or throwing the ball toward the bowling pins.

What about an object that is already moving? According to Newton's law, if an object is moving, it will continue to move forever until some force makes it stop. Take for example when you kick a soccer ball. The ball moves through the air, and Newton says, it will continue to move until something stops it. Well, gravity will pull the ball down toward the ground, but then the ball will begin rolling. The ball will continue to roll, until another force (the ground) makes it stop. The ball may get caught in a water puddle, get tangled in the grass, or get slowed down as it rolls over rocks. The ground in this case is providing a force called friction to make the ball slow down and eventually stop.

Newton's Second Law of Motion: The acceleration (how velocity changes) is related to the strength of the force and inversely related to the object's mass. What does this all mean exactly? Well, this law is saying that the ability to speed up an object or slow down an object depends on two things: the force and the mass of the object. Take a car for example. Cars are heavy or have a high mass, this means, it is harder to change the velocity of a car, unless a great force is applied. Likewise if you have a very light object, it would be easy to change the object's speed and a small amount of force can do so.

Newton's Third Law of Motion: For every action, there is an equal and opposite reaction. This is the idea that forces come in pairs. Think about swimming. As your hand pushes through the water, the water pushes back on your hand. According to Newton, if one force or action is happening in one direction, then there is an equal force or action happening in the opposite direction. As long as the forces are equal then the object does not move. For example, if the water is pushing with a force of 10 Newtons (Note: Newtons is the unit of measurement for force. The larger the number, the larger the force on the object), then your body would be pushing with an equal force of 10 N against the water. If instead, the forces are not equal, let's say there is a large wave in the pool and the water is now pushing against you at a force of 20 N, but your body is still pushing with the same 10 N against the water, the water has the larger force and will be able to move you.

Motion is an important part of the universe and motion can occur when objects are attracted to another and also when objects are repelled. Let's now dive into magnets!

What Is Magnetism?

Magnetism is a type of force that can cause motion. Magnetism is created by electricity. But what causes electricity? Small particles within objects called electrons help to create electricity. Within every object, there are small spheres called atoms. Within an atom is a smaller sphere that is called the nucleus. Around the nucleus are electrons that move in circles or orbits around the nucleus. This is similar to how the Earth moves around the Sun! Electrons have a negative charge and they spin either up or down. In most objects, the number of electrons that spin upward are equal to the number of electrons that spin downward. When this happens they cancel each other out. However, in some objects like iron, the electrons spinning upward are not equal to the electrons spinning toward, and these extra electrons can attract other objects, like metals.

Magnetic objects are all around us! There are even magnetic objects in outer space. The Sun and Earth are very magnetic, because there spins of the electrons are not equal. Deep inside the core of the Earth is a dense ball of iron metal. It is this metal core that allows compasses to work and find North.

There are naturally magnetic rocks called lodestones. For thousands of years, people made magnets using lodestones. It is not clearly understood exactly how lodestone became to be magnetic. Some scientists believe that lodestone became magnetic after having been struck by lightning.

How Do Magnets Behave?

If you have ever experimented with magnets, you may have observed a very peculiar behavior. Magnets have poles or ends. Just like Earth, magnets have a North and South Pole. If you place two magnets together, they can either attract each other, or repel each other. This is where the statement "opposites attract" is important. Magnetics placed together with opposite poles (South and North or North and South) touching will attract each other. On the other hand, magnets with the same pole (North and North or South and South) touching will repel each other.

Magnets can be made using elements found on Earth, like iron, aluminum, nickel, or cobalt.

Activities

Try these fun experiments to learn more about motion and magnets!

#1 – I spy something…magnetic!

Materials:

- 2 large plastic cups or containers
- 4 magnets of different sizes and shapes
- 1 paper plate or flat surface
- 10-15 items such as bouncing balls, plastic toys, metal toys, paper clips, crayons, magnetic pieces, erasers, etc.

Procedure:

1. Label four of the cups with the words "Magnetic" and four of the cups with the words "Not Magnetic".

2. One by one, place each of the items on the paper plate and use each magnet (one at a time) to pick up the object.
3. If the magnet can pick up the object put it in the magnetic cup. If not, put it in the not magnetic cup.

What's happening?

Magnets have an unequal number of spinning electrons. This makes them very attracted to metals. When you place a magnet near something that has metal, the magnet will attract or stick to it. When you place the magnet near something that does not have metal, the metal seems to not do anything and will not stick to the object.

#2 – Magnetic power

Materials:

- 3 plastic containers with lids

- Pipe cleaners (have different sized ones)

- 3 magnets of various sizes and shapes

Procedure

1.) Before starting the experiment, you should cut the pipe cleaners into smaller pieces. You can make them however long or short you like 1 inch pieces work best.

2.) Add the strands into the containers and close the lid. Be sure to keep the different size strands separated.

3.) Place a magnet somewhere on the container (the top is usually best) and slightly shake the entire container.

4.) After the container has been shaken, the pipe cleaner strands should be sticking to the container where the magnet was placed.

5.) Carefully count the number of strands that stuck to the magnet. You may need to take the lid off and count them outside of the container.

What's happening?

Magnets have invisible force fields that make them attracted to metals, just like the metal that is found inside the pipe cleaners. The power, or force, of the magnet is strong enough that it can pass through some materials, like the plastic of the container or lid.

#3: Round and round

Materials:

- Penny

- Balloon

Procedure:

1. Place the penny inside of the balloon. The balloon should NOT be blown up.

2. Carefully blow up the balloon, making sure that the penny stays in the balloon.

3. Tie the balloon closed.

4. With the penny inside of the inflated balloon, begin to move the balloon in a circle. Going faster and faster each time.

5. The penny should begin to travel around the inside of the balloon in a circle.

6. Stop moving the balloon and the penny should keep moving!

What's happening?

The penny was at rest before you started moving the balloon. When you applied a force, moving the balloon in a circle, the penny moved. The penny continued to move even after you stopped moving the balloon until gravity pulled it down. Remember Newton's first law of motion: "An object at rest will stay at rest, and an object in motion will stay in motion, unless acted upon by an outside force."

#4: The Card and the Penny

Materials:

- One playing card

- Small cup (plastic is best)

- A quarter

Procedure:

1. Place the card on top of the cup.

2. Put the quarter on top of the card.

3. Very quickly pull the card straight out from under the coin.

4. Watch what happens to the coin!

What's happening?

The quarter wants to not move, this is called inertia. When the card is moved the inertia is greater than the movement of the card, so the quarter remains in the same spot, even if the card is not there. Without the card, there is nowhere for the quarter to go expect inside of the cup.

#5: Vanishing Colors

Note: This experiment requires **adult supervision.**

Materials:

- Liquid white glue

- 12 inch Ruler

- Pencil

- String

- Scissors

- 4" x 4" piece of cardboard

- Paper plate

- One plastic cup

Procedure:

1. Cut the entire edge off of the paper plate. You should be left with a circle.

2. On the circle, trace the opening of the cup and cut it out.

3. Using the ruler, divide the circle into six equal sections.

4. Color the circle a different color in each section.

5. Trace a circle on the cardboard, using the opening of the cup and cut this circle out.

6. Glue the colored circle to the cardboard.

7. Ask an adult to make two holes in the center of the circle.

8. Lace the string through the two holes and tie the ends of the string together.

9. Move the string in a circular motion to wind it up.

10. Hold the string firmly, one piece in each hand, and pull tight and watch the wheel of colors spin!

11. Where did all the colors go?

What's happening?

The colors on the wheel seemed to disappear. This is because the fast movement of the wheel made all the colors blend together and make it seem as if they were not there at all.

Quiz

Check Your Understanding

1.) _____ is all around us and is an important part of physics.
2.) True or false. Objects move based on force.
3.) What is velocity?
4.) If a car is accelerating, then it is _____.
5.) If a car is decelerating, then it is _____.
6.) True or False. The mass of an object does not influence its motion.
7.) Movement in a curve or random path is called _____ motion.
8.) Movement in a straight path is called _____ motion.
9.) _____ was an English scientist that studied the laws of motion.
10.) True or false. An object in motion will automatically stop.
11.) True or false. An object at rest will stay at rest.
12.) Force is measured in what unit?
13.) Magnetism is created by _____.
14.) Give two examples of magnet objects (not including magnets).
15.) True or false. The quartz rock is a natural magnet.
16.) True or false. Magnetism happens when the number of electrons spinning one way is equal to the number of electrons spinning another way.
17.) The ends of a magnet are called _____.
18.) Opposite _____ of a magnet attract each other.
19.) Identical poles of a magnet _____ each other.
20.) Name an element that can be used to make a magnet.

Quiz Answers

1.) Motion is all around us and is an important part of physics.
2.) True. Objects move based on force. Forces can be you pushing or pulling on an object, but it is needed to cause motion or movement.
3.) Velocity is similar to speed; it is how fast an object is moving.
4.) If a car is accelerating, then it is speeding up.
5.) If a car is decelerating, then it is slowing down.
6.) False. The mass of an object does influence its motion. Think of it this way…the larger the object the harder it will be to move and the more force you will have to apply to move it.
7.) Movement in a curve or random path is called complex motion.
8.) Movement in a straight path is called simple motion.
9.) Sir Isaac Newton was an English scientist that studied the laws of motion.
10.) False. An object in motion will remain in motion unless acted upon by an outside force. Gravity is the force that usually causes objects to stop moving.
11.) True. An object at rest will stay at rest unless acted upon by an outside force. This is Newton's first law of motion.
12.) Force is measured in Newtons or N.
13.) Magnetism is created by electricity (or electrons).
14.) The Earth and the Sun were two examples of natural magnets mentioned in the section.
15.) False. The lodestone rock is a natural magnet.
16.) False. Magnetism happens when the number of electrons spinning one way is not equal to the number of electrons spinning another way. If the numbers are equal, the electrons "cancel" themselves out. With magnets all of the electrons are not canceled out.
17.) The ends of a magnet are called poles.
18.) Opposite poles of magnets attract each other. Like if you were to put the South pole of one magnet near the North pole of another magnet, they would attract or come together.
19.) Identical poles of magnets repel each other.
20.) Iron, aluminum, nickel, or cobalt are elements that can be used to make magnets.

Life Science #1: Reproduction and Genetics

Life can be a mysterious process. How exactly is life formed? In this section we will go through some of the basics of reproduction and how traits are inherited or passed on from one generation to the next. At the end of this section you will have the opportunity to explore inheritance much more with some activities that involve studying and learning more about your family's traits.

What Is Reproduction?

Reproduction is the process that organisms go through to create new organisms or offspring. There are two different types of reproduction: asexual and sexual.

Asexual Reproduction is when one organism splits into two, forming an exact copy of itself. Humans do not reproduce this way, but bacteria do. This is a very quick and easy process but does not allow for a lot of variety. Think if it this way, if you were to create a copy of yourself and then your copies create more identical copies, there would be a lot of "you" running around. Copies that all look, act, and think the same way.

Sexual Reproduction is when two organisms have to come together and share material. This involves the mating of a male and a female. The male has sperm which carries the important information for the father and the female has eggs that also carry important information but from the mother. The egg and the sperm have to meet and the sperm has to go inside of the egg. When this happens, the sperm's information or DNA and the egg's information or DNA mix together to make a baby that has a mixture of the two pieces of DNA. Now, this is where there can be lots of variety. Based on the information that each parent gives the child will determine how the child looks and what traits the child can have and pass on to their children, when they have them.

Sexual reproduction is not as fast as asexual reproduction because it involves more organisms (2 instead of 1) and after the egg and the sperm meet, the baby has to grow inside of the mother or inside of an egg. For example, you grew inside of your mother's womb for 9 months after the egg and the sperm met and a baby bird has to grow inside of an egg for 2 weeks before it can hatch.

Why Is Variety Important?

In nature, the more variety or differences we have the more likely we can adapt to different things. If everyone were to look and behave the exact same way, what could we really learn from each other? Not much. If all the birds looked the same, ate the same things, and lived in the same area, it would be hard for them to survive as food ran out or space became limited. If the environment should change, it is much harder for identical organisms to live. Even if we all have very little differences, that is still variety. Variety allows us to adapt.

What Is Adapting?

What do you do if you are cold? You may shiver, put on a coat, or get a blanket. You are adapting or trying to deal with the cold temperature. Animals and plants have to adapt all the time. There are some things like the temperature that are outside of our control and all we can do is try to adapt the best way we can. Some animals are able to better adapt than others. The polar bear can live in very cold environments because it has a thick layer of fat that protects it from the cold and keeps warm. Humans don't have this, so we would likely not survive in a very cold environment without having some source of heat, like a fire. Animals are able to adapt based on what traits they have. These traits are passed on from their ancestors and are traits that help the animal to live. Take the giraffe for example its long neck was developed over hundreds of years as they had to stretch farther and farther up into the trees for leaves. Those giraffes that inherited the long neck from their parents were better able to survive until all giraffes had a long neck. In many cases, organisms are different because of mistakes or mutations that happen inside of the organism's body.

What Are Mutations?

Inside of our body we have cells. There are millions of cells in our body and they are responsible for keeping us alive. Inside of our cells is a special structure called the nucleus. The nucleus is like a bank vault, it stores the treasure of the cell which is the DNA. DNA is like a recipe, it has all of the information to know how to make cells, which cells to make, which body parts to make and when, even what we will look like. As cells divide, the DNA has to be copied so that each new cell has their own copy. When the DNA is copied mistakes happen by accident. Think about when you may type or write something and you have a typo. A mutation is like a typo. It is done randomly and in some cases does not affect anything, but in other cases, the mutation may change the entire DNA recipe. Mutations happen all the time, in every organism. Mutations also help to give variety to make sure everyone's DNA recipe is slightly different. Many times mutations can be a helpful thing and can give an organism a new, special trait that helps it to survive better. Let's look at an example.

Roaches are an annoying and gross bug. They can usually be killed with rock spray. If you use rock spray on a roach, it is likely to die, but some may live. Why is that? Some roaches may have a mutation that changed their DNA recipe to allow them to live even if they are sprayed with roach spray. Now, this mutation may not work on every single type of roach spray, but it does help them survive some of the roach sprays. Scientists would say that the roaches have become *resistant* meaning they can resist dying.

We see the same thing in humans. Have you ever had to take antibiotics? Antibiotics are designed to kill bacteria like if you have an ear infection or strep throat. They usually work to kill most bacteria, but sometimes you may get infected with bacteria that are resistant to the antibiotic. This is because the bacteria may have a mutation to allow it to live even if you are taking antibiotics. Like with the roach example, the mutation will not allow the bacteria to resist all antibiotics, so switching to a different antibiotic may kill the bacteria.

These resistances are able to be passed on when the organism reproduces.

What's A Trait?

For this section we will define a trait as a physical characteristic. You may have the trait for blue eyes, or the trait for curly hair. Traits are passed on from generation to generation. Traits that are harmful or make it harder for an organism to live are usually eliminated over time. So, the traits we have should be able to help us survive and adapt to our environment.

What does "passed on" mean?

The traits we have like eye color, skin color, height, hair texture, even diseases are inherited from our parents. This means that the DNA recipe from your mother and the DNA recipe from your father mixed together to create you. Depending on how they mixed together will determine important physical traits about you. Your parents' traits came from the mixture of their parents DNA, just like your children's traits will come from the mixture of your DNA and your future husband or wife's DNA. Some traits are dominant and may occur more often. Brown eyes are an example. Other traits are recessive and in general may not occur more often. Colorblindness is an example of a recessive trait.

Some traits run in families. You may notice that all the members in your family are tall or they all have blond hair. In this case, the trait for tallness runs in your family. When people with different traits have children this creates lots of variety. For example, a man with black hair and brown eyes may have a child with a woman with brown hair and green eyes. They may have a son with black hair and green eyes and a daughter with brown hair and brown eyes. The way the parents DNA and traits mix is completely random, so there are a lot of possible combinations of what traits the children can inherit. It is also possible to have children that have the same physical characteristics as one of the parents. This does not mean that the child is identical to the parent because remember the child's DNA recipe is made from their mother and their father, not just one parent. So, on the outside the child may look like their mother or their father, but if we were to dive into their cells and look at their DNA recipes, they would be different. Identical twins are the only two types of people that will have identical physical characteristics and identical DNA recipes.

Activities

Test out your understanding of traits and inheritance with these eye-opening experiments!

#1: Who Has What?

For this experiment you will need to talk to at least 5 other family members.

Materials:

- Pencil and paper
- 5-8 family members

Procedure:

1. On a piece of paper, make a table with 6 columns and 8 rows.
2. On the far left column write the statements below, one in each box going down the side of the paper.

I have attached earlobes

I can roll my tongue

I have dimples in my cheeks

My hair is naturally curly

I cross my right thumb under my left thumb when I clasp my hands

I have freckles on my skin

I write with my right hand

I have food allergies

3. At the top of the second column, write your name.
4. For each statement, write yes or no in the second column.
5. Find other family members and have them repeat step 4, putting their responses in the other columns.
6. Look at the traits of your family members. Do you all have the same traits? Are there any ones that are different?

What's happening?

Traits are passed on from your parents. Even if you have the same parents as your siblings, you could have inherited different combinations of traits. For example, you could have dimples, attached earlobes and be right handed, but your brother could be left handed. IN nature, there is no one way of inheriting traits, it is done randomly, so the combinations of traits that a child can get from their parents are endless!

#2: Can you taste it?

Materials:

- PTC paper (this can be bought on the internet)
- 5-10 people (can be family members)

Procedure:

1. If the PTC paper is not already cut into strips, cut the paper into long thin strips.
2. Place the paper on your tongue and observe the taste.
3. On your paper mark "yes" if the taste of the paper is bitter or mark "no" if you do not taste anything.
4. Find 5-10 other people, can be family members and repeat steps 1 through 3. Keep track of how many "tasters" and how many "non-tasters" there are.

What's happening?

About 75% of people can taste the bitter taste of the paper, while 25% may not taste anything. The ability to detect the bitter taste is something you inherited from your parents. A scientist discovered that the types and strength of our taste buds depends on what we inherit from our parents.

#3: Who do you look like?

Materials:

- 7 plastic containers

- permanent marker

- Small colored blocks or objects (6 of each color - red, yellow, blue, green)

- Paper and pencil

Procedure:

1. Label each of the container as follows: Grandfather 1, Grandmother 1, Grandfather 2, Grandmother 2, Father, Mother, Child

2. Mix up the colored blocks and without looking choose 6 blocks and put them in the container marked Grandfather 1.

3. Repeat step 2 for the Grandmother 1, Grandfather 2, and Grandmother 2 containers.

4. Write down how many colors are in each container.

5. Without looking choose 3 blocks from Grandfather 1 and place it in the Father container.

6. Without looking choose 3 blocks from Grandmother 1 and place it in the Father container.

7. Write down how the colors and how many of each are in the Father container.

8. Without looking choose 3 blocks from Grandfather 2 and place it in the Mother container.

9. Without looking choose 3 blocks from Grandmother 2 and place it in the Mother container.

10. Write down how the colors and how many of each are in the Mother container.

11. Without looking choose 3 blocks from the Father container and place it in the Child container.

12. Without looking choose 3 blocks from the Mother container and place it in the Child container.

13. Write down how the colors and how many of each are in the Child container. How do the child's blocks compare with their grandparents? Or their parents?

What's happening?

This is how traits are passed on. They are passed on randomly from what is there to choose from. You didn't look when choosing the blocks, so the combinations of blocks likely changed as you went through the experiment. This is how traits change over time and are passed on within our families. In some cases, two people can have the same colored blocks. This is true in real life as well. Sometimes family members can have the same characteristics, like twins or triplets, it's rare, but it happens!

#4: What's inside?

Materials:

- Resealable plastic bag

- Fresh strawberries (3-4 large ones)

- Dish washing detergent

- Measuring spoons

- Salt

- Water

- 2 clear plastic cups

- Filter (a coffee filter works fine)

- Rubbing alcohol

- Wooden stick (popsicle sticks work great!)

- Measuring cup

Procedure:

1. Remove the leaves from the strawberry.

2. Place the strawberries into the plastic bag, seal, and carefully smash them.

3. Measure 2 teaspoons of dish washing detergent and 1 teaspoon of salt and place it in the plastic cup.

4. Measure ½ cup of water and pour it into the plastic cup with the salt and detergent.

5. Take 2 teaspoons of the liquid from the cup and carefully add it to the bag with the mashed strawberries. Reseal the bag.

6. Gently mix the contents in the bag with your fingers. Try not to make too many soap bubbles in this step.

7. Place the paper filter on the empty plastic cup.

8. Pour the strawberry solution through the filter.

9. Pour about ½ cup of rubbing alcohol down the side of the cup over the strawberry solution.

10. Use the wooden stick to scoop up the cloudy white substance that forms on the side of the cup. This is the strawberry's DNA!

11. If it didn't work this time, try it again with one of the other strawberries you have left.

What's happening?

You have found the DNA of the strawberry! DNA is a special part of all living things, this is the "recipe" that tells our bodies how to grow, how they will look and what traits we can pass on to our children. DNA is the most important thing in our body's cells because without it our body would not know how to function. What you pull out on the wooden stick is the important information for the strawberry. This white, cloudy material has all the information on how to grow the strawberry, when to have it ripen, even when it will rot and die.

#5: What color are your eyes?

Note: For this experiment you will need to talk with your grandparents, parents, and siblings. If you cannot talk with your grandparents, ask your parents to help.

Materials:

- Large white poster board

- Pens, pencils and markers (green, gray, blue, brown)

Procedure:

For this experiment you will be tracking the eye colors throughout your family.

1. Make a family tree, similar to the image below, using circles to represent the people.

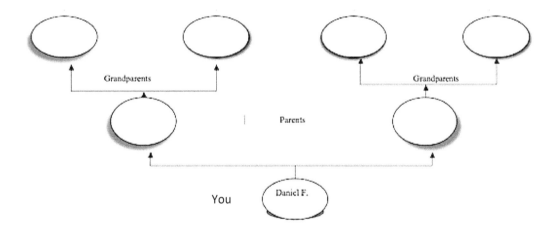

2. Ask each family member what their eye color is and color their circle with that color. If you're able, ask your grandparents about their parents' (your great grandparents) eye color.

3. You should end up with a family tree that has different colors for you to track how the eye color in your family is passed from one generation to the next.

What's happening?

Traits like eye color are passed from your parents to you. You may notice that your whole family has the same eye color or you may see that there are lots of different eye colors in your family. Your eye color is determined by the traits that your mom and your dad have and how they mix together. Since our genes are not always seen by looking at a person, it is not uncommon for two people to have a child that has a different eye color from both of the parents!

Quiz

1.) What are the two types of reproduction?

2.) _____ reproduction is when an organism splits into two organisms, both being identical.

3.) Which type of reproduction happens the fastest?

4.) True or False. Sexual reproduction involves two organisms.

5.) What is inside of the nucleus?

6.) Why is DNA important?

7.) What is the definition of a trait?

8.) How are traits passed on?

9.) What is a mutation?

10.) True or False. A mutation is an intentional change in the DNA recipe.

11.) Why do animals need to adapt?

12.) Give an example of a trait.

13.) Mutations provide _____.

14.) True or False. Having a lot of variety is bad for the population.

15.) Give an example of a recessive trait.

16.) Give an example of a dominant trait.

17.) Which type of trait, dominant or recessive, occurs more often?

18.) _____ have identical copies of DNA.

19.) How can a child and a parent look the same but have different DNA recipes?

20.) When you have children your DNA recipe will mix with what?

Quiz Answers

1.) The two types of reproduction are asexual and sexual reproduction.
2.) Asexual reproduction is when an organism splits into two organisms, both being identical.
3.) Asexual reproduction happens the fastest because one organism can split into two organisms.
4.) True. Sexual reproduction involves two organisms, one male and one female.
5.) The DNA or DNA recipe is inside of the nucleus.
6.) DNA has all the information of how to grow the organism, what they will look like, and what traits they will have.
7.) For this section, we defined a trait as a physical characteristic.
8.) The DNA recipes of the parents is mixed together and this determines what traits are passed on and what traits the child will have.
9.) A mutation is a change in the DNA recipe. This happens when the DNA is copied.
10.) False. A mutation is an accidental change in the DNA recipe. Most mutations are never noticed and some can allow the organism to have a new and helpful trait that it didn't have before.
11.) Animals have to adapt to their environment in order to be able to survive.
12.) Answers may vary. In this section height, skin color, eye color, and hair texture were given as examples of traits.
13.) Mutations provide diversity or variety.
14.) False. Having a lot of variety is good for the population. The more variety the more likely organisms can change and adapt to their environment.
15.) Having colorblindness is an example of a rare and recessive trait.
16.) Brown eye color is an example of a dominant trait.
17.) Generally dominant traits occur more often than recessive traits. There is one important exception. Dwarfism is a dominant trait. So, in this case everyone who is not a dwarf is recessive, meaning dwarfism does not occur very often.
18.) Identical twins have identical copies of DNA.
19.) Physical traits can be the same, but the DNA recipe can be different depending on how the DNA recipes of the person's parents were mixed together.
20.) When you have children your DNA recipe will mix with your husband or wife's DNA recipe to determine what traits your child will have.

Life Science #2: Life cycles

Another characteristic of living things is that they grow and change over time. You can think of how this happens in terms of a life cycle. For plants the cycle goes like this: A seed lands in a place where it can grow—somewhere where it has soil, sunlight, and water—and it germinates, or begins to sprout. It grows small roots; then tiny leaves break through the soil. The plant continues to grow, getting larger and producing more leaves. When it is fully grown, it can produce seeds of its own—often from a flower—and the cycle begins again when the seed is pollinated and drops or is carried from the plant.

Animals go through life cycles too, although the cycle may start in different ways. There are three phases of life for animals: before birth, young, and adult. Let's explore each phase.

Before birth – depending on the animal this phase can take place inside of an egg or inside of the mother's womb. Some babies hatch from eggs. Insects, fish, amphibians, reptiles, and birds (and a few mammals) start out life this way. During this phase, important structures like the brain, the heart, the backbone, and the organs form. Most animals look the same during this phase, since most animals need the same important parts to survive. The time spent in this phase varies greatly depending on how long the mother is pregnant. For a cat, pregnancy lasts about 2 months. For a human, this phase would be about 9 months long, but for an elephant, the mother is pregnant for almost 2 years!

Young – this phase could last 1 day to 18 years. Some animals like the deer or the horse expect their young to be able to walk and run immediately after birth. Whereas monkeys nurture their young for years before letting them leave and live on their own. Bears send the young off to the wild alone after one year with their mother. Many reptiles are expected to find their own way immediately after hatching and will never be nurtured during this phase. During this type, there is rapid growth of the body. Reproductive structures like the ovaries in females and the testes in males will continue to grow but will not be fully developed to have babies.

Adult – this part of life is characterized by being able to reproduce. This is the stage in life when an animal is able to have its own young. For some animals, this stage is not reached for over 10 years, for other animals, this may be reached within 1 year or less. During the adult phase, the animals body may continue to grow though much slower than it did in the young phase. At the end of this phase is death. Though death can be a scary thought, it is a natural part of life. An animal can die in any phase of the life cycle and most animals are more likely to die in the before birth and young phases than any other phase. For the adult animal, especially those entering "old age" their mental and physical abilities begin to break down and they may behave like an animal in a much young phase of life. For example, an older gorilla may not be able to walk as far, which is very similar to the same physical limits of a young gorilla. The life expectancy for an animal varies greatly. Humans have an average life expectancy of about 75 years, an elephant can live for 70 years, a crocodile for 50 years, and a tortoise can live for over 100 years!

Plants and animals live finite lives that may last hours or many years, but they all die. Reproducing ensures that others will take the place of those that die.

Let's look at the life cycle of some interesting animals.

How does life begin for amphibians?

Amphibians, like frogs have a somewhat complex life cycle. Unlike other types of animals, they go through a big change called a metamorphosis. This means that the animal in the young phase will look very different than the animal in the adult phase. Generally amphibians are born either hatching from eggs or from their mother's womb, then they live during the young phase in the water. Since amphibians are able to live on land **and** in the water they have to have gills (for the water) and lungs (to breathe on land). The tricky part is that the gills and the lungs cannot develop at the same time. The gills will develop first, so the young frog or tadpole will spend most of its childhood in the water breathing with gills. As the tadpole grows, it begins to lose some of its body parts like the tail and the gills will be replaced with lungs. As the adult frog, it will now spend most of its life on land.

Scientists say that frogs go through a partial metamorphosis because the young and the adult phases are only slightly different. Let's look at an organism that goes through a complete metamorphosis.

Insects

These creatures are amazing because their young stage looks nothing like their adult stage. They completely change in a very short period of time. We will look at the life cycle of a butterfly.

What are the stages of the lifecycle of a butterfly?

There are four stages for the butterfly's life cycle. They are: the egg, the larva, the pupa, and the adult.

The egg – is the unborn stage. In this stage the eggs are laid by the female butterfly. She will generally lay her eggs on plants. The plants will be the food source for the growing butterfly when it hatches from the egg as the caterpillar.

The female butterfly lays eggs in the every season, except for the winter. The exact egg-laying time depends on the species of butterfly. During each laying, hundreds of eggs are released. Butterfly eggs are very, very small. There is a high chance that most eggs laid will not become butterflies, so the female lays as many eggs as she can in the hopes that at least some will grow, hatch, and survive.

The larva – After the egg has been laid, the next stage is the larva stage. The "baby" emerges from the egg and is called a caterpillar. The main job of the caterpillar is to eat as much as it possibly can. The caterpillar will eat and eat and grow and grow during this stage. The caterpillar will grow so much that it will have to split and shed its skin at least 4 times. As the caterpillar eats the food is stored for it to use in later stages.

Did you know a caterpillar can grow over 100 times bigger than it was when it first hatched? Most caterpillars are the size of a pen tip when they first hatch but can grow to be 2 inches long within the matter of 2 weeks!

The pupa – The caterpillar will enter this stage after it is full grown and has eaten all it can eat. For butterflies the pupa is called a chrysalis. The chrysalis may attach under a branch, bury itself underground, or hide in leaves. Different species of butterflies spend this stage in different ways. During this stage, the cocoon is formed to protect the growing pupa. This stage could last up to a month! Some species are known to be in this stage for two years!

This is when the metamorphosis or the big change occurs. Parts of the pupa will grow very quickly to make the wings, legs, and eyes of the adult butterfly. The stored food from the larva stage will be what the pupa lives off of as it grows inside of the cocoon.

The adult – After all of the growing is done, the butterfly will emerge from the cocoon, completely transformed! The butterfly looks nothing like the egg, or the caterpillar that it came from. The caterpillar is almost blind, with few eyes and has short legs and short antennae. The adult butterfly is the exact opposite. It has many eyes with great sight, long legs and antennae. Butterflies spend their time flying and eating nectar from plants. There are some butterflies that do not eat at all and instead continue to live off of the food they stored as a caterpillar. But, butterflies do not continue to grow! They stay the same size during the adult stage.

In this stage, the butterflies main job is to mate and lay eggs to make new butterflies. The female adult butterflies will fly from branch to branch looking for the right spot to lay her eggs to start the cycle all over again. She has to be sure to find the right spot, so when the eggs hatch they have lots of food nearby.

Butterflies have a very short life span. Most only live two or three weeks. Some butterflies are able to live through the winter by hibernating and these types of butterflies can live for several months.

Do all insects go through a complete metamorphosis?

No. In fact some insects like the grasshopper and cockroaches go through an incomplete metamorphosis. This means that they do not go through the pupa stage and their life cycle is a bit simpler.

These insects have: the unborn stage or the egg, the young stage called the nymph, and the adult stage. During the nymph phase they eat as much as possible and grow very rapidly. In the adult stage the growing slows dramatically, wings form, and the insects main focus becomes mating and laying eggs to start the cycle all over again. Like insects that undergo complete metamorphosis, these insects' life spans are also very short lasting no more than a few months.

Animals are amazing and grow in many different ways. In the next section, you will learn about how plants grow and develop!

Activities

Try these fun science activities to learn more about animal development.

#1 – Wormy becomes a butterfly

Materials:

- Caterpillar (this can be purchased online, if not found outdoors)
- Terrarium with lid
- Plant materials

Procedure

1. Place the plant materials into the terrarium.
2. Carefully add the caterpillar.
3. Be patient and watch as the caterpillar eats and eats and eats for several days.
4. Eventually it will form a chrysalis and emerge as the beautiful butterfly!

What's happening?

The caterpillar moves through the life cycle towards becoming a butterfly. In this case, though, the students actually get to see them transform during each stage.

#2: Growing Fruit Flies

Materials:

- Sliced fruit (apple, banana, and grapes)

- Clear plastic container with plastic lid

- Knife

Procedure:

1. Ask an adult to cut several slits in the plastic lid with the knife.

2. Place the sliced fruit in the container.

3. Let the container sit in a well-lit corner for several days.

4. Voila, you've made fruit flies!

What's happening?

Fruit flies are amazing little creatures. They have special sensors to find the smell of ripened and rotting fruit. They are so small that they can easily creep into your home when they smell fresh fruit nearby. Once they find the rotting fruit, they lays eggs, sometimes on the fruit itself and start to make other fruit flies. If you're not careful, you'll have thousands of fruit flies before you know it! The life cycle of a fruit fly is less than 8 days. They can go from an unhatched egg to full grown adult in about a week's time. Amazing, right?

#3: Here come the maggots!

Materials:

- Plastic container with lid

- Raw fresh meat (steak or beef is best)

- Small plastic container

- Corn meal (optional)

Procedure:

1. Place the raw meat in the large plastic container and seal with the lid.

2. Place the container outside in a sunny area and leave for 1.5 days.

3. Carefully take the lid off and leave it off. This is not the best smell, but it's great to attract flies!

4. Leave the container uncovered and outside for another 1.5 days.

5. After 1.5 days, seal the container and bring it indoors and put in a shady and cool place. You can also leave it outside in a shady place where animals won't disturb it like an outdoor window sill.

6. Wait for a few days and maggots should start to hatch in the container on the raw, decaying meat.

7. If you transfer the maggots to the small plastic container and give them corn meal, they will eat and eat and eat and then form the pupa, just like a caterpillar forms the chrysalis.

What's happening?

When the meat is outdoors covered it begins to decompose from the heat of the sun. When it is left uncovered, female flies detect the smell and lay their eggs on the meat. Meat and decaying matter is a great place for fly eggs since the maggots that emerge will have lots to eat. When you put the container in a cool, shady place, you allow time for the eggs to hatch and the maggots to appear. With this experiment you are experiencing the fly life cycle first hand!

#4: To the Ant maze!

Note: This experiment requires an **adult's assistance and supervision.**

Materials:

- Two glass jars, one large with lid and one small. The small jar should be able to fit inside of the large jar

- Ants and dirt

- Cotton balls

- Water

- Honey

- Dark colored paper

Procedure:

1. Place the small glass jar upside down inside of the large glass jar. In other words, the bottom of the small glass jar should be facing upwards.

2. **With an adult's help,** locate an ant hill and carefully dig up some of the dirt and capture some of the ants.

3. Ask an adult to make holes in the large glass jar's lid.

4. Transfer the soil and the ants to the large glass jar, filling the space between the two glass jars.

5. Place the lid on the large glass jar and cover the entire jar with brown or dark-colored paper.

6. Soak 3 cotton balls with water, placing a drop of honey on each cotton ball.

7. Put the cotton balls in the large glass jar.

8. Wait a few days and you'll see the ant's begin to tunnel.

What's happening?

Ants are very hard-working bugs. When the paper is wrapped around the jar, it mimic them being underground. Like many animals that live in the soil, ants burrow and make tunnels to travel from the surface of the ground, collecting food, to go back to the ant's nest deep in the soil. The small glass inside of the large glass takes up a lot of space, so the ants are forced to make their tunnels against the walls of the large glass, which makes it really easy for you to see all of their hard-work!

#5: What...bacteria?

Materials:

Bread

Resealable bag

Water

Procedure:

1. Soak the bread in water, until the bread is semi-soaked.

2. Place the bread in the resealable bag and seal.

3. Leave the bread in a warm place for 3-5 days.

4. Observe what starts to grow on the bread.

What's happening?

The bread starts to form mold which is a type of bacteria. Did you know that bacteria were the first organisms on Earth? Scientists have discovered that the first bacteria came from microorganisms that were made by the combination of dirt, gases in the air, and lightning. If is from bacteria that over millions of years, animals and plants slowly evolved.

Quiz

Living things _____ and _____ over time.

1.) Name the three phases of life for animals.
2.) When does most of the growing happen? During what phase of life?
3.) True or False. Death is a natural part of life.
4.) Name two animals that may hatch from an egg.
5.) What happens during the adult phase of life?
6.) Define the phrase *life span*.
7.) Name an animal with a short life span.
8.) Name an animal with a long life span.
9.) Name an animal with a short pregnancy period.
10.) Name an animal with a long pregnancy period.
11.) True or False. Amphibians go through metamorphosis.
12.) Name the stages of the butterfly's life cycle.
13.) What is the difference in the life cycle of a butterfly and the life cycle of a grasshopper?
14.) What is the main job of the adult butterfly?
15.) True or False. Adult butterflies eat a lot during this time.
16.) What does the word metamorphosis mean?
17.) What does the female butterfly have to consider when she lays her eggs?
18.) Why does the female butterfly lay hundreds of eggs at a time?
19.) What happens during the before birth phase of life?

Quiz Answers

1.) Living things grow and develop over time.

2.) The three phases of life for animals are: before birth, young, and adult.

3.) The most growing happens in the young phase, this is when the animal begins to develop from being very small at birth to being much larger at the end of this phase.

4.) True. Death is a natural part of life. During the adult phase, animals reproduce to leave more animals even after their death to continue the life cycle.

5.) Birds and reptiles like snakes and crocodiles hatch from eggs.

6.) During the adult phase growing slows down and the adult's main job is to reproduce and raise offspring.

7.) Life span is how long an animal is likely to live. For some animals this is a very short time, for other animals this is a long period of time.

8.) The butterfly has a short life span. They are expected to live about 2-3 weeks.

9.) The tortoise has a long life span. They can live to be over 100 years old.

10.) A cat has a short pregnancy period of about 2 months.

11.) An elephant has a long pregnancy period of almost 2 years.

12.) True. Amphibians, like the frog go through metamorphosis. It may not be a complete metamorphosis like the butterfly who changes their entire physical appearance, but amphibians are said to do a partial metamorphosis.

13.) The stages of the butterfly's life cycle are: egg, larva (caterpillar), pupa (chrysalis), and adult (butterfly).

14.) The life cycle of a butterfly is an example of complete metamorphosis and has 4 stages and the life cycle of a grasshopper is an example of an incomplete metamorphosis and only has 3 stages.

15.) The main job of the adult butterfly is to reproduce and lay eggs.

16.) False. Adult butterflies do not eat at all during this time. They live off of the stored food that the caterpillar ate during the larva stage.

17.) Metamorphosis means "big change".

18.) The female butterfly has to consider where she lays her eggs and how close the location is to a food source. Caterpillars cannot travel long distances and need to have an immediate food supply after they hatch from the egg.

19.) Not all eggs will hatch and not all caterpillars will develop into a butterfly. The adult female butterfly lays hundreds of eggs hoping that at least a few will develop into butterflies to start the life cycle all over again.

20.) During the birth phase of life there is rapid growth of important structures like the heart, the brain, muscles, and bones.

Life Cycle #3: Plant Development

Like animals, plants also have a life cycle and stages of development. Plants begin their lives as a tiny seed or spore and have to find oil to get nutrients and begin to grow their roots, stems, and leaves.

The green algae is considered to be the ancestor of plants. It was from the green algae millions of years ago that all of the plants we have today came from. There are four types of plants: bryophytes, seedless vascular plants, gymnosperms, and angiosperms. Some of these plant groups are very simple, while others are more complex.

Bryophytes – they are also known by their common name, "moss". These plants have to be near water and cannot grow to be very tall. They reproduce by releasing spores into the air. The spores are then carried by either water or wind and eventually fall to the ground and sprout into more moss. These are the simplest of all plants.

Seedless vascular plants – a fern is an example of this type. These are more complex than the mosses but are not the most advanced plants. These plants can grow to be much taller than the moss because they have a vascular system. What is a vascular system? A vascular system is like your blood vessels in your body. It is a network of channels that helps to carry nutrients and water throughout the plant. This allows plants to be able to grow tall and strong. There is a special channel called the phloem that carries sugars and other nutrients from the plant's leaves down throughout the rest of the plant. There is another special channel called the xylem that carries only water. The xylem carries water from the roots of the plant up through the stem to the plant's leaves.

The seedless vascular plants like the ferns were the first plant to have a vascular system. Ferns reproduce using spores, like the mosses do. This is not the best way to reproduce because a lot of the spores dry out or get washed away and never sprout into new plants.

Gymnosperms – this is a fancy word for "cone-bearing" plants like the pine tree. These are much more complex than the other two plant groups. The pine tree has a vascular system like the ferns and is able to grow very, very tall. Gymnosperms were the first plant group to have seeds not spores. The seeds are in a protective covering called the cone. Pine trees drop their cones and hope that animals will pick it up and bury it for the in topsoil, with enough water and sunlight for it to grow into another tree.

Angiosperms – these are the most complex of all the plant groups. Angiosperms are flowering or fruit-bearing plants like the apple tree or like a rose. These plants also have a vascular system to transport nutrients and also use seeds to reproduce. They also have scents or bright colors to attract pollinators like bees and other insects. For a flower, the pollinator, say a bee, would land and get the nectar from the flower. Some of the plant's pollen would rub off onto the bee. When the bee then leaves and lands on another plant, the pollen would brush off and go into the new plant, helping to fertilize the egg to make a new flower plant.

How does a plant grow?

For plants to grow whether from spores or seeds, they have to absorb enough water. This is important because a seed will stay dormant (meaning will not grow) if there is not enough water in the environment. This is a way for the plant to ensure that there are enough nutrients in the area to help it grow and stay healthy. If there is enough water, the seed will absorb water and then begin to germinate or sprout. Some seeds will not sprout unless they are exposed to very high temperatures like in a fire. Amazingly, after a forest fire, there will be new plants that sprout. That is because they were "awaken" or begin to sprout only **after** they have experienced extreme heats. This helps the forest rebuild itself and grow over time.

Now, let's learn about what plants need to survive.

All plants need soil, water, carbon dioxide (a special kind of gas released from humans), and sunlight. Plants are autotrophs; this means that they can automatically make their own food as long as they have all the things they need. Plants need to make a sugar called glucose. They use sunlight, water, and carbon dioxide to make glucose in a process called photosynthesis. If plants do not have enough water or sunlight, they cannot make their own food and then would starve.

Plants are an essential part of the ecosystem. Plants, including trees, produce oxygen when they go through photosynthesis. Oxygen is needed by humans and animals to survive. Plants and animals form an interesting circle, where plants carbon dioxide from humans and animals, and humans and animals need oxygen from plants. This is why it is devastating when trees and plants are destroyed.

What are the parts of the plant?

Plants have leaves, a stem, and roots. The plant leaves are where photosynthesis happens. This is because the plant's leaves are exposed to the most amount of sunlight. There are special structures in the plant leaf that absorb sunlight and allow for photosynthesis to happen. During the day, plants store as much light as they can in their special structures called chloroplasts and can even do photosynthesis at night when it is dark.

If the glucose (or sugar) for the plant is made in the leaves, how does it get to the rest of the plant? Well, the stem is important in transporting nutrients. You can think of the stem as a highway connecting the leaves to the rest of the plant. In the stem is the xylem which carries water and the phloem which carries the sugars and other nutrients from the leaves to other parts of the plant. The stem grows longer and longer over time to make sure that the leaves are getting enough sunlight.

The roots drill deep into the ground to access water. In some plants like grass, the roots are very wide and not very deep. These are called fibrous roots. For plants with these kinds of roots, the water is near the top of the soil, so the plant's roots do not have to go far into the ground to get the water it needs. For other plants, like a carrot, the root has to go very far down into the ground to get to the water. This long type of root is called a taproot. Taproots are very important during times of drought when the amount of water in the soil may be low. These roots can grow further down through the topsoil to get to water that may be trapped beneath the soil.

Do plants move?

Because plants have very strong roots, they are anchored in place. Plants do not move like animals do and cannot leave if the environment does not have enough nutrients. Plants can however respond to the environment by growing or bending in certain ways.

A plant can bend or grow its stem in one direction if there is more sunlight on one side. For example, if there is more sun on the right side of the plant, it can cause the left side of the stem to grow more, allowing the plant to curve and lean more to the right side to reach the sunlight.

Other plants like ivy can grow toward another plant or an object. For some plants, they continue growing until they touch something. This something could be a tree, another plant, a fence, even a building. Ivy grows toward whatever it is touching. This is why you might see ivy wrapped around a tree, on a gate, or on the side of a building. Some plants grow away from objects or other plants. The petals of a flower can close if touched. This is a way for the plant to try to protect itself.

Plants even respond to gravity. In the growing seed, it can determine which direction the roots have to grow based on gravity. The roots always grow in the same direction with gravity (down) and the stem always grows in the opposite direction of gravity (up).

What is the life cycle of a plant?

Some plants have one life cycle that lasts about one year. These are called annuals and have to be replanted each year. Corn and wheat are examples of annual plants. Other plants are biennials, meaning they have their life cycle lasts two years or two growing seasons. Parsley is an example of a biennial. Lastly, there are perennials. These plants have a much longer life cycle and can be planted once and come back each year. Examples of perennials include lavender, petunias, and lilies.

Activities

Try these interesting plant activities and experiments to learn more about plants, their parts, and what they need to grow.

#1 – Ready, Set, Grow!

Materials:

- Styrofoam cups

- Water

- Plant seeds

- Soil

- Sunlight or bright light to mimic sunlight (a plant lamp works great!)

Procedure

1.) Fill the cups about halfway with soil.

2.) Place the plant seeds into the middle of the soil.

3.) Carefully pour enough water to dampen the soil. Not too much!

4.) Put the cups on a window sill or under the plant light.

5.) Water the plant a little every day and take notes of what you see happening. Be patient! Plants have to do a lot of growing underground, so you may not see anything for a few days.

What's happening?

The seed will sprout when it has enough water. Once the seed sprouts, it will need the light to help it to produce its own food through a process called photosynthesis.

#2 – The light! The light!

Materials:

- Soybean plants (they should be about the same size)

- Fertilizer

- Soil (potting soil is fine)

- Water

- Colored filters or colored transparency sheets (clear, red, green, and blue)

- Very large plastic container (at least 18 – 24 inches in length, 8-12 inches deep, and 6 inches wide)

Procedure:

1.) In the large plastic container, evenly place potting soil. The soil should be 5" deep.

2.) Plant 4 of the soybean plants in 5" of moist potting soil.

3.) Read the fertilizer directions and put in the recommended amount of fertilizer.

4.) Place a different colored filter over each soybean plant. They can be draped over the sides of the container or taped in place.

5.) Place the aquarium in a place that will receive a lot of direct sunlight.

6.) Water the plants each day and take notes about what you see happening and how much each is growing.

What's happening?

Because light gives the plants the energy it needs to create its own food (photosynthesis), the color of the light can be very important. This experiment shows the relationship between light and plant growth.

#3 – Milk, Juice, Soda, and Water…Oh My!

Materials:

- Seeds (green bean seeds work the best!)

- 5 small plant pots

- Potting soil

- A measuring cup

- Whole milk

- Apple or orange Juice

- Soda (any kind is fine)

- Sports Drink like Gatorade or Powerade

- Water

- Black permanent marker

Procedure:

1. Label each plant pot using the black permanent marker. They should be labeled as: "Water/Control," "Juice," "Soda," "Juice," and "Sports Drink."
2. Fill each pot with potting soil about halfway up.
3. Plant three seeds in each of the pots.
4. Measure ½ cup of each liquid and pour it in the plant pot labeled with that liquid. For example, water goes in the "Water/Control" pot, milk goes in the "Milk" pot, etc.
5. Place the pots in a warm, sunny place outdoors or on a sunny window sill indoors.
6. Each day water the plants with the liquid they should get and keep track of their growth.

What's happening?

We know that plants need sunlight, nutrient-rich soil, and water to grow. Although it best for the water to be clean and clear, some plants can grow even when the water is polluted or has a high salt content. Understanding what types of fluids that can help plants grow helps scientists learn more how to help plants and people in times of draught.

#4: The Changing Flower

Materials:

- 3 white carnations

- 3 plastic cups

- Food coloring (you'll need red, green, and blue)

- Water

- Scissors or knife

Procedure:

1. In each of the three plastic cups, fill them halfway with cool water.

2. Place 3-5 drops of food coloring in each cup. For example, place 3 drops of red in one cup, 3 drops of blue in one cup, and 3 drops of green in one cup.

3. Cut the very end of the carnation stems (you should only cut off about ¼ inch of the stem).

4. Place one carnation in each cup and leave for 45 minutes.

What's happening?

The plants roots and stems absorb water. The water travels to the plants leaves and petals. With this experiment the colored water was absorbed and the colors appeared in the petals of the carnation as the water traveled up from the roots through the stem to the top of the plant.

#5: Amazing Clay Plant Balls

Materials:

- Clay (modeling clay is best)

- Wax paper

- Potting soil (you can get this from your local hardware or gardening store)

- Plant seeds

Procedure:

1. Soften the clay by kneading it with your hands.

2. Flatten the clay and make it into a small circular disc. This should have a 4-6 inch diameter.

3. Put a small handful of potting soil on top of the clay.

4. Place a few plant seeds on top of the soil.

5. Fold the clay so that the potting soil and seeds are on the inside of the clay.

6. Roll the clay into a ball. The soil and seeds should now be in the inside of the clay ball.

7. Place a handful of soil and the remaining seeds on a flat surface and roll the clay ball over them. They should start to stick on the outside of the clay ball.

8. Set the clay ball on the wax paper and leave for 2 days, or until the clay has dried out.

9. Plant the clay ball in your backyard and watch the plants grow!

What's happening?

Some environments are very dry and this makes it very hard for seeds to sprout and grow. By having the soil and seeds mixed with clay allows the moisture and water to stay and keep the seeds healthy. The soil inside of the seed ball is a food source for the growing seeds inside of the ball. The seeds will be protected inside of the clay until there is enough rainwater to wash the clay away and allow the seed to sprout and grow into a plant.

Quiz

Check Your Understanding

1.) What are the three plant groups?
2.) What plant group does not have a vascular system?
3.) What is a vascular system?
4.) True or False. The xylem carries water throughout the plant.
5.) True or False. The phloem carries nutrients and sugars up from the roots to the leaves.
6.) Which is the most complex plant group?
7.) What is a seed?
8.) Name the three parts of the plant.
9.) _____ is like the plant's highway to transport nutrients.
10.) Give an example of a plant that grows toward touch.
11.) _____ _____ is the ancestor of all plants.
12.) What will happen if one side of the plant is exposed to more light than the other side?
13.) Plants are autotrophs which mean they _____ _____ _____ _____.
14.) True or false. Plants go through photosynthesis to make their own food.
15.) Name at least 3 things plants need to survive.
16.) The _____ grow in the same direction as gravity.
17.) The _____ grows in the opposite direction as gravity.
18.) What is the difference between a fibrous root and a taproot?
19.) How long is the life cycle of a biannual?
20.) True or false. A perennial has to be replanted each year.

Quiz Answers

1.) The three plant groups are the bryophytes (moss), the seedless vascular plants (ferns), the gymnosperms (cone-bearing plants), and the angiosperms (fruit-bearing plants).

2.) The bryophytes or mosses do not have a vascular system. Since they cannot transport nutrients throughout the plant, they do not grow very tall.

3.) It is a way for plants to transport nutrients and water throughout the plant. The vascular system is made up of the xylem and the phloem.

4.) True. The xylem carries water throughout the plant.

5.) False. The phloem carries nutrients and sugars, but it carries it down from the leaves through the rest of the plant to the roots. The xylem runs in the opposite direction, carrying water up from the roots to the plant's leaves.

6.) The angiosperms or flowering/fruit-bearing plants are the most complex plant group.

7.) A seed is a protective covering where the growing plant lives until it sprouts to form a new plant.

8.) The roots, stem, and leaves are the three parts of the plant.

9.) The stem is like the plant's highway to transport nutrients. It is inside of the stem where the xylem and phloem are.

10.) An ivy or a vine is an example of a plant that grows toward other objects or toward whatever it is touching.

11.) The green algae is the ancestor of all plants.

12.) The plant will make its stem longer on the side opposite the light so that the stem can bend toward the light.

13.) Plants are autotrophs which mean they make their own food.

14.) True. Plants go through photosynthesis to make their own food. This happens in the leaves where they are exposed to sunlight.

15.) Plants need water, soil, carbon dioxide, and sunlight to survive.

16.) The roots grow in the same direction as gravity.

17.) The stem grows in the opposite direction as gravity.

18.) A fibrous root is wide, not deep. This is for plants that do not need to drill down deep in the soil for water. However, a taproot is long and is needed for plants that have to go deep into the soil to access water.

19.) The life cycle of a biannual last two growing seasons or two years.

20.) False. A perennial does not have to be replanted each year. An annual plant like corn or wheat has to be planted each year. Perennials are able to live for more than two growing seasons and may need to be replanted every 3-5 years.

Earth Science #1: Rocks

Did you know that there are different types of rocks? In fact, there are three different types of rocks: sedimentary, metamorphic, and igneous. We will go through each type of rock in this section. It is important to remember that rocks can start of as one type of rock, but over the course of thousands of years, can change into another type of rock. We will discuss this rock phenomenon throughout this section.

Sedimentary Rock

Sand, broken shells, and smaller rocks or pebbles form what is called sediment. Over time, the sediment builds up in layers and then starts to harden to form rock. Since the sediment are different types of materials with different size particles and textures, sedimentary rock is relatively soft and is very brittle. This is the type of rock where fossils can be found. We'll talk a lot more about fossils in a later section. Limestone is an example of sedimentary rock.

Sedimentary rock gives rise to coal and petroleum. Over three-quarters of the Earth's surface is covered in sedimentary rock.

Metamorphic Rock

In science the term metamorphosis means to undergo a change. Metamorphic rock is formed within Earth and is made by exerting extreme pressure and heat. These types of rocks appear to be shiny and are made very slowly. Marble is an example of metamorphic rock.

Igneous Rock

Deep within the layers of the Earth is a layer called the mantle. The mantle contains magma which is a super-hot liquid substance. Magma can come to the Earth's surface, like during the eruption of a volcano, and cool to form rock. Magma can also cool without coming to the Earth's surface. When magma hardens in the crust, it forms a type of igneous rock called granite. Granite takes a long time to cool, but when it does, it is very hard and not easily broken. Most mountains are made of this type of igneous rock.

This type of rock is characterized by looking like glass and often has pockets of gas trapped inside the solid structure. These gas pockets leave tiny holes in the cooled rock. Basalt or volcanic rock is an example of igneous rock.

Mountains are an interesting phenomenon as it relates to rock and rock formation. New mountains are often tall and have jagged edges along its surface. Over millions of years, new mountains turn into old mountains, which are more rounded and shorter in height. Why do mountains shrink? The rock on the mountain gets worn down through a process called rock erosion. We'll talk more about rock erosion later in this section. The bits of rock that are lost or chipped off from the mountain form the sediment that then can be combined to create sedimentary rock. So, igneous rock from mountains, can then be made into sedimentary rock millions of years later.

The layers of Earth are made of rocks. The outermost layer, the crust, has a top layer made of soil, sand, broken rocks, and water. Digging deeper into the crust, you will find rocks of all types. Right below the soil layer (where we plant and dig) is a solid layer of rock called bedrock.

What is the rock cycle?

Rocks have a life cycle, just like animals do. They are formed, worn down, broken, and reformed all the time. The rock cycle is hundreds, if not thousands of years long. There are six steps of the rock cycle. We will go through each.

Step 1: Weathering and Erosion

What is weathering? Weathering can either be a physical process or a chemical process. During physical weathering pieces of rock are broken down to form sediment. Chemical weather, on the other hand, involves the dissolving of minerals within the rock, changing the composition of the rock altogether.

What is erosion? Think of it this way…everything in nature wears down over time. Just like our bodies and muscles may wear down as we age, so too do rocks. Erosion is a necessary part of the rock cycle as this is what provides sediment to then form sedimentary rock. Rock erosion can be dangerous, especially if large boulders chip off of a mountain's surface or if the rock that supports a house wears down. The good thing is rock erosion takes a long time to occur, as the rock is exposed to rain, hot and cold temperatures, and wind.

Step 2: Rock Transport

Once erosion has occurred, rock particles (sediment) may be moved by wind, animals, or some form of water like rain, streams or oceans. These rock particles begin to accumulate near one another and begin to set the stage for new rock formation.

Step 3: Deposition

The sediment is able to travel, in some cases, very far distances, until they settle and begin to collect. Sediment then starts to mix with soil and forms a new layer of sediment. Over time, these groups of floating layers of sediment can create rock islands.

Step 4: Compaction and Cementation

Layers of sediment can stack on top of one another, causing pressure to build up one the lower layers. This pressure can force the sediment particles to come so close together that they are able to form new solids. The spaces in between neighboring sediment particles are often filled with dissolved minerals, like calcium to make the new rock. Since this rock is made by compacting sediment together, this is how sedimentary rock is formed.

Step 5: Metamorphism

Sedimentary rock can be formed deep within the Earth's layers under thousands of tons of other rocks.

The more these rocks get forced deeper into the ground the more pressure put upon them and the higher the temperature is around them. This extreme pressure and heat can change the shape of these rocks from being sedimentary to metamorphic rock. Eventually these rocks get pushed so deep into the Earth's crust that they go into the hot mantle or magma and are melted.

Step 6: Rock Melting

Rocks can actually melt! This is true when metamorphic rocks are pushed into the magma. When rocks melt, they become part of the super-hot magma, which can then go to the Earth's surface and cool to make igneous rock. This starts the rock cycle all over again!

Special Types of Rock Formations

Have you ever been inside of a cavern? In caverns there are special rock formations made from minerals like calcium. There are some rock formations that emerge from the ceiling and grow down toward the ground. These are called stalactites. Other rock formations emerge from the ground and grow tall toward the ceiling. These are called stalagmites. There is an easy way to remember which rock formation is which by looking at the names of each. Stala**c**tites have a "c" in their name, which will help you remember that they are on the **c**eiling. Whereas stala**g**mites have a "g" since they start on the **g**round. These types of rock formations can also be called dripstones because they are made from water moving calcium deposits. As the water "drips" from the tips of these rock formations, it adds more calcite (a special form of calcium) to the growing formation. This process takes thousands of years to happen!

 What about precious stones?

Some rocks are considered to be precious stones or gems. These are rare crystals made of minerals. Depending on the type of mineral, the gem may look different and have different shapes. For example, diamond is made of a collection of carbon, whereas rubies are made by the mineral corundum.

Some precious stones are very hard and not easily broken. Diamond is the hardest of the gems. Other precious stones are very brittle such as emeralds. Precious stones have to be harvested or dug up from the ground. In some cases, people may dig with shovels and screen or sort through the soil to find precious stones. In other instances, people may do cave mining and travel into caves, breaking the walls to find precious stones that may lie beneath the rock's surface. The rarity and the quality of the precious stone helps to determine its value. Very rare stones like Tanzanite, a blue-purple colored stone are found only near Mount Kilimanjaro, in Northern Tanzania. This makes it very rare and very valuable, especially to jewelers.

The Hope Diamond is the most famous precious stone in the world. It is not your average diamond. Instead, the Hope Diamond is blue-white in color. It is so rare that it is kept in a museum in Washington, D.C.

As you have learned in this section, rocks can come in a wide variety of shapes, sizes, and colors. Rocks are not as boring as they may appear because rocks are always changing and going through the rock cycle. Starting a rock collection is a fun and easy way to study rocks like geologists do! Rocks hold a wealth of information about the past and about the composition of Earth. We can find fossils in some types of rocks and even learn about past animal and plant life. Next time you pick up a rock, think about where it came from and what it may become thousands of years from now.

Activities

Try these cool rock experiments to test your understanding of rocks, the types, and the rock cycle.

#1- Chart that rock!

Materials:

- Poster board or large sheet of white paper

- Black marker or pen

- Sticky notes

Procedure:

1. In the center of the poster board, draw a large circle. Around the circle draw 5 straight lines coming from the circle.

2. Draw multiple lines coming from the circle.

3. Using the sticky notes, write one fact you learned about rocks and place it at the end of each line. If you can think of more than 5 facts about rocks, draw more lines and keep going!

What's happening?

When you learn a new concept, it is important to reflect on what you learned and write it down. This activity should get you thinking about what you do know and what you have learned about rocks. Keep this in your room as a reminder of all the cool and interesting things you know about rocks!

#2 – Sand, Pebbles, and Glue—Oh My!

Materials:

- Sand

- Small rocks or pebbles

- Liquid glue

- Large clear plastic cup

Procedure:

1) Place a thin layer of sand in the bottom of the cup.

2) Pour the liquid glue into the cup and then add several of the small rocks. Be careful not to add too much glue, though, because the rocks will take longer to dry.

3) Repeat steps 1-2 until the cup is about 2 inches full.

4) Place the cups in a window sill (with lots of sunlight) for the cups to dry.

5) After a week, the materials should be dry.

6) With an adult's help, cut the cup away and, voila, you have your very own rock!

What's happening?

The sand, small rocks, and glue bond together to form a solid object, much like the rock you might see in the backyard.

#3 - Why kick rocks when you can eat them?!

Note: This experiment requires **adult assistance and supervision**.

Materials

- Aluminum foil

- Wax paper

- Starburst candy

- Toaster oven

- Towels

- Flat surface

Procedure

1.) Unwrap the Starburst candy.

2.) Lay the aluminum foil flat on the table and place the square of wax paper on top.

3.) Stack the 3 different Starburst in the middle of the squares

4.) Wrap the papers around the Starburst tightly, making sure to mold the foil around the shape of the Starburst.

5.) Because sedimentary rocks are made by pressure over time to "make" a sedimentary rock formation apply pressure. This can be done by squishing the Starburst with your hands or pressing it down against the table.

6.) Metamorphic rocks are made by heat and pressure. To make metamorphic rocks ask an adult's help to wrap the Starburst in foil and place it in the toaster oven for approximately 2 minutes or until the Starburst is soft but not melting. Then, wrap the "rock" in a towel and apply pressure. After the "rocks" have cooled and been pressed, remove the foil and wax paper to see your new metamorphic rock!

7.) Igneous rock is created from extreme heat. To make igneous rocks, the Starburst (wrapped in wax paper and foil) should be placed in the toaster oven on high heat for about 5-10 minutes. The Starburst should be melting but not burnt when it comes out of the oven. Once it is melted, ask an adult to carefully open the foil and wax paper and take a quick peek. Let the candy cool.

What's happening?

You are able to see how the three different types of rock are formed from start to finish. Seeing the different "rock" pattern by using candy is a great and yummy way to better understand what each rock type looks like and why they look that way.

#4: Deep Freeze!

Materials:

- Rocks, like limestone, granite, and sandstone (these can be found at your local hardware or gardening store)

- Empty plastic water bottle

- Water

Procedure:

1. Examine the rock. Take a note of its size and shape.

2. Place the rock in the water bottle.

3. Fill the bottle with water and place the lid on it.

4. Put the water bottle in the freezer for 6 hours.

5. Take the water bottle out and let it thaw out.

6. Repeat steps 3 and 4 at least three more times.

7. Carefully take the rock out and look at it. What has changed?

What's happening?

Remember that rocks get broken down or erode over time by being exposed to the wind, the rain, and by hitting other rocks. Rocks are also weathered by being frozen and then thawing. When a rock freezes, the water seeps into the small cracks in the rock and as the water turns into ice, it expands. This causes even bigger cracks in the rock. When the rock thaws and the ice melts, the rock has larger spaces than it did before. The process keeps continuing until pieces of the rock completely break off.

#5: The Absorbent Rock

Materials:

- Chalk

- Water

- Cup

Procedure:

1. Place one piece of chalk in the cup.

2. Fill the cup with water.

3. Let sit for 24 hours.

4. Carefully pour out the water. What do you notice about the chalk?

What's happening?

Rocks are solid, but they do have small cracks or openings in them. These openings can allow rocks to absorb water. These are called porous rocks and chalk is one of these types of rocks. Chalk is made up of calcium carbonate, similar to an egg's shell. The chalk is able to absorb water, it takes time, but it is a type of natural rock sponge.

Quiz

Check Your Understanding

1.) Name the three different types of rocks
2.) What type of rock is formed under extreme heat and pressure?
3.) Sand, broken shells and smaller pebbles make _____.
4.) What is an example of igneous rock?
5.) _____ is a super-hot liquid substance in the Earth's mantle.
6.) Mountains are which type of rock?
7.) What is the difference between a new mountain and an old mountain?
8.) What is below the soil layer?
9.) Rocks are formed, worn down, and reformed during the _____.
10.) What is rock erosion?
11.) How are rock pieces transported?
12.) What is weathering?
13.) Name the six steps of the rock cycle?
14.) What occurs during the cementation step of the rock cycle?
15.) True or False. Rocks can undergo melting.
16.) Name the rock structure that is attached to the ground of a cavern and grows to the ceiling.
17.) Name the rock structure that is attached to the ceiling of a cavern and grows to the ground.
18.) Diamond is made of _____.
19.) Name three types of precious stones.
20.) What is the most famous precious stone?

Quiz Answers

1.) The three types of rock are: sedimentary, metamorphic, and igneous.

2.) Metamorphic rocks are formed under extreme heat and pressure. This often occurs in the mantle of the Earth which is a super-hot liquid type substance.

3.) Sand, broken shells and smaller pebbles make sediment.

4.) Granite is an example of an igneous rock.

5.) Magma is a super-hot liquid substance in the Earth's mantle.

6.) Mountains are a type of igneous rock. They are formed when magma reaches the Earth's surface and is cooled.

7.) New mountains are tall and have jagged sides. Old mountains because of rock erosion over time are shorter and more round/smooth.

8.) Bedrock is below the soil layer. This is a solid layer of rock.

9.) Rocks are formed, worn down, and reformed during the rock cycle.

10.) Rock erosion is when rocks are worn down over time. This can happen because they are exposed to rain and wind and can also happen when rocks are under extreme pressure.

11.) Rock pieces that break off during rock erosion are often transported by the wind and water.

12.) Weathering is the natural breakdown of rock. This can be due to physical or chemical processes.

13.) The six steps of the rock cycle are: weathering and erosion, rock transport, deposition, compaction and cementation, metamorphosis, and rock melting.

14.) The rock pieces or sediment is forced together and begins to form one large piece of rock.

15.) True, rocks can melt. This is one of the steps of the rock cycle and this occurs when the rock is pushed into the hot magma in the Earth's mantle.

16.) Stalagmites are attached to the ground of a cavern and grow toward the ceiling.

17.) Stalactites are attached to the ceiling of a cavern and grow toward the ground.

18.) Diamond is made of carbon.

19.) Three precious stones are: diamonds, rubies, and emeralds.

20.) The Hope Diamond is the most famous precious stone. It is owned by the Smithsonian museum in Washington, D.C.

Earth Science #2: Soil

You just learned about rocks and when they break down to smaller pieces called sediment. Sediment is an essential part of what forms soil or dirt. When rocks continue to break down into smaller and smaller pieces, this forms sand. Sand particles are very tiny.

Plants can sprout in sandy areas and as plants die and are broken down by bacteria, these "stuff" mixes with the sand to form soil. Soil is necessary for life on Earth. Plants could not live without having soil and water for their roots. Likewise, there are a lot of animals that could not live without plants, and this would trickle all the way up to humans.

What are the many names of soil?

You may call soil, "dirt". Soil can also be called clay, silt, or humus. Wet soil forms mud. Soil is located on the outermost part of the Earth, along the crust. There are many layers of soil, with some layers being more nutrient rich for the plants to get nutrients and other layers may be nutrient poor.

Have you ever heard of topsoil? Topsoil is the layer of soil that has the most nutrients for plants to use. Gardeners often buy topsoil from hardware stores and use it in their gardens to help give their plants the nutrients they need to grow and be healthy. Soil is made up of varying amounts of minerals and living and dead matter.

What's living matter?

The soil is the home to plant roots, small insects like caterpillars or ants. These are considered living matter as they are alive and grow. Many organisms call the soil home because it is often damp, cool, and a great place to burrow or hide from predators.

What's dead matter?

Death is a part of the natural life cycle of animals and plants. When a leaf falls from a tree, it will land on the surface of the soil and over time, it will break apart and decompose. The nutrients that were in the leaf will now get absorbed by the soil and these nutrients can then be reabsorbed or used by other plants in the soil. When an animal dies, the same process occurs. The animal's body decomposes and releases important nutrients into the soil for other organisms to use to grow.

Fungi like mushrooms and bacteria are important in helping to break down dead matter to recycle their nutrients. Bacteria are also important in taking nutrients from the air such as nitrogen and converting it into a form that can be absorbed in the soil. This is similar to what fertilizers do. Fertilizers provide soil with important nutrients like nitrogen if there is not enough in the soil already.

How is soil made?

Plant roots are an important part of making soil. As plants' roots grow deeper into the soil, sometimes breaking through rock, more soil is made. Roots also cause the soil to be loose and not compacted together. This benefits insects and animals living in the soil as it allows them spaces to move and travel in the soil, but it also allows for oxygen to enter the soil. Oxygen is an important gas that animals (and humans) need to survive. If the soil was too tightly packed, it would squeeze out all of the oxygen, making it impossible for animals and insects to breath.

What nutrients are needed in the soil?

Plants rely on the soil to give them the nutrients they need to grow. What do you think would happen if the soil does not have any more nutrients for plants? The plants would eventually die. Plants are sessile, meaning they cannot move. So, if there are no nutrients (or not enough) for them in their current location, they cannot get up and move like animals can. In order for plants to be healthy, they need:

Nitrogen – This is an important nutrient found in fertilizers and this helps leaves and stems to grow. Leaves are the structures the plant uses to make its own food. Without them, the plant would starve. The stem helps the plant to grow toward the Sun. The Sun and light are essential to a plant's development. In order to make its own food, a plant needs the sunlight to start the process. This is similar to you needing a fire on the stove to cook pasta. Without the fire, the pasta wouldn't cook.

Phosphate – This nutrient helps fruits and roots to develop. Roots are needed to help the plant dig deep into the soil to find water. Water is such an important substance in all animal and plant life.

Potassium – This helps to maintain plant health. Plants do not need large amounts of potassium, but without even small amounts, plants could die. Some plants like bananas store potassium in large amounts and bananas are a great source of potassium for humans and animals!

What are the layers of soil?

Soil forms layers also called horizons. There are three soil horizons: topsoil, subsoil, and bedrock.

Topsoil – This is the upper layer of soil. When you touch the ground, you are touching the top soil layer. This is the layer where plants get nutrients like nitrogen, phosphate and potassium to grow. This layer of soil is easy to spot. It is often a very dark brown color and may contain dead and decaying matter such as leaves, dead plants, etc. In order for the topsoil to remain rich in nutrients dead matter must be added and decayed. Remember soil itself is not alive, so it cannot make nutrients on its own. Instead, the plants depend on other things like fallen plants and leaves and dead animals to decompose and recycle their nutrients into the topsoil.

Subsoil – if you dig deeper, past the topsoil layer, you will hit the subsoil. This layer looks more like clay and is important for storing water for plants. A plant's roots will begin in the topsoil layer, but grow deep into the ground into the subsoil to get to the water. The subsoil can be moved or washed away very easily through erosion, so it is important that it stays covered by the topsoil layer.

Bedrock – This is the lowest layer of soil. You would have to dig at least 3 miles into the ground to hit bedrock. In some places, you may have to dig even further down past the top two layers of soil to get to this layer. Bedrock can also be called the parent layer because this layer as it breaks down and moves upward forms the subsoil and also the topsoil layers.

Knowing the different soil layers is part of the battle. Soil can be classified based on the types of particles within it. Take for example clay soils. This type of soil has a lot of small particles and not a lot of nutrients, making this the least suitable type of soil for plant growth. In addition, clay soils are so tightly packed that there is no room for oxygen to be stored in the soil and there is little to no water. Sandy soils have a lot of large particles. This leaves very large spaces in the soil for oxygen or water to be stored. In comparison to clay soil, sandy soil can be good for plant growth since there is water and oxygen present within the soil.

What is soil erosion?

You learned about rock erosion earlier. The same process can happen to the soil. When it rains, the topsoil can be carried by the rain water and collect in other places like in streams, rivers, and oceans. When the soil moves, it may take key nutrients with it. Think about what would happen if your house was built on a hill. Over time, the soil from the hill may be washed away and your house could be in danger of sliding off of the hill. This phenomenon is often referred to as a "landslide" or a "mudslide". When nutrients levels in the soil are low, rainfall can leave the remaining soil without any nutrients for the plants to use. This is what occurs in the tropical rainforest. The tropical rainforest is home to thousands of exotic plants and animals, but also has the worse soil. This is because of the high amount of rainfall. Every year, the tropical rainforest has almost one foot (12 inches) of rainfall. That's a lot of rain! With every rainfall, more and more of the nutrients in the topsoil are washed away.

Here are some interesting soil facts:

1.) Soil has been an influential part of everyday life for millions of years. It has been used to make food, clothing, medicines, even paper! In some ancient civilizations, mud from the soil was used to build homes.

2.) Each year millions of tons of soil is eroded or washed away.

3.) Farmers can help to keep soil healthy and full of nutrients by rotating crops. This means that one year a farmer may plant corn, but the next year he/she may plant wheat. Because plants are different, different crops will use different amounts of nutrients. By changing the crop every year or every two years, farmers can make sure that the levels of important nutrients stay high.

Activities

#1 – Soil, Soil Everywhere

Materials:

- Clay soil

- Soil loam

- Sandy soil

- Plastic cups or jars

- Coffee filters

- Rubber bands

Procedure

1. Set out three cups or jars.

2. Attach coffee filters to tops of the cups or jars using rubber bands.

3. Place the different soils on different jars. For example, one for clay soil, one for sandy soil, and one for soil loam).

4. Pour water over each of the soils to see what happens to the water as it passes through each type of soil.

What's happening?

The water is absorbed better by the soil loam, which means that it is a better soil for planting.

#2 Yummy Soil!

Materials

- Clear plastic cups (larger cups are better for this project)

- Paper plates

- Marshmallows (small to medium size)

- Cheerios

- Chocolate rice crispies

- Mini M&Ms

- Gummy worms

Procedure

1. Put marshmallows in the very bottom of the cup because it will represent the bedrock.

2. Cheerios should be the next layer, representing the subsoil. You can put in whole Cheerios or mash them up.

3. Above the Cheerios will be the chocolate rice crispies with mini M&Ms mixed in. The rice crispies represent the topsoil and the M&Ms represent humus.

4. To finish, add in a couple gummy worms.

What's happening?

Looking at all of the layers of soil can be difficult because the layers can be hundreds of feet deep. Using these ingredients help us see what the layers look like, without having to dig hundreds of feet into the ground. Plus, it is tastier this way!

#3: Soil Mix-Up

Materials:

- Soil (this should be from your backyard)

- Two large glass jars with lids

- Spoon

Procedure:

1. Fill one glass jar one-third of the way full with soil.

2. Fill one glass jar with clean water.

3. Add the water from the jar in step 2 to the jar from step 1, until the soil and water jar is almost full.

4. Use the spoon to mix the soil and water mixture.

5. Leave the jar for one hour. What do you see? Can you see the contents of the jar? Are there different layers?

What's happening?

When the jar is left undisturbed the contents in the soil starts to separate. The bottom layer is where the sand is since it has the largest sized particles. Silt will be on top of the sand layer. If there was clay in the soil, then that would be on the top layer. The water at the very top will not be clear because it will have decaying plant material also called organic material.

#4: No Dirt Needed!

Materials:

- Sweet potato

- Glass cup

- Water

- Toothpicks

Procedure:

1. Put three toothpicks into the sweet potato, in the large end. The toothpicks should stick out in all directions.

2. Take the glass cup and fill it more than half way with water.

3. Put the sweet potato into the water with the end with the toothpicks sticking up and resting on the opening of the glass jar. The toothpicks should be holding the sweet potato upside down into the glass.

4. Place the glass cup in a sunny place and leave for at least 3 days.

5. Watch the vine grow from the sweet potato without using water!

What's happening?

Some plants, like the sweet potato can grow without nutrients from the soil. The sweet potato is able to live off of the sugars it made during photosynthesis. These sugars give the plant the energy it needs to sprout into a plant.

#5: Who's There?

Materials:

- Soil (this works best with soil from your yard)

- Glass jar with lid

- Lime water (this can be purchased at a grocery store)

- Small dixie cup (this needs to be able to fit inside of the glass jar

Procedure:

1. Place a few handfuls of soil into the glass jar.

2. Fill the cup with lime water.

3. Place the dixie cup into the jar, resting it on top of the soil.

4. Seal the glass jar with the lid and let the jar sit untouched for 2 days. What do you see?

What's happening?

The lime water changed from being a yellowish clear liquid to milky white. Why is that? There are small organisms that live in the soil. Most you can't see with your eyes, you'd have to use a microscopic. These organisms breathe in oxygen and release carbon dioxide. The carbon dioxide mixed with the lime water to turn it to a milky white color.

Quiz

1.) How is soil formed?

2.) True or False. Sand particles are very large.

3.) What are two other names for soil?

4.) What are the layers of soil?

5.) Which layer of soil has the most nutrients for plants?

6.) True or False. The subsoil layer stores water.

7.) Give an example of living matter.

8.) _____ help to break down dead animals and plants to give nutrients to the soil.

9.) A plant's roots can break through _____ to form more soil.

10.) _____ is important because it helps the leaves of a plant form and develop?

11.) True or False. Without phosphate the fruit on a fruit tree would not grow.

12.) What layer of soil is made up of clay?

13.) If you dug 3 miles down into the ground, you would hit the _____ layer.

14.) Name the layer of soil that erodes or gets washed away very quickly.

15.) A mudslide can occur when what happens?

16.) Name three things that we get from the soil.

17.) True or False. The tropical rainforest has the most nutrients in its topsoil.

18.) Framers can keep the topsoil healthy by _____ _____.

19.) What causes soil erosion?

20.) What organism needs soil the most?

Quiz Answers

1.) Soil is formed when bits of rocks and decomposing matter are broken down.
2.) False. Sand particles are very tiny.
3.) Soil can also be called dirt, humus, clay or silt.
4.) There are three layers, they are: topsoil, subsoil, and bedrock.
5.) The top layer or the topsoil has the most nutrients for plants. This is where nutrients from dead leaves and animals are absorbed.
6.) True. The subsoil layer stores water.
7.) Answers may vary. Living matter is anything that is alive. This can include plants, insects, and animals.
8.) Bacteria help to break down dead animals and plants to give nutrients to the soil. Fungi are also important with breaking down dead matter as well.
9.) A plant's roots can break through rock to form more soil. This is what actually helps to form new soil.
10.) Nitrogen is important because it helps the leaves of a plant form and develop? Nitrogen is often in fertilizers for this very reason.
11.) True. Without phosphate the fruit on a fruit tree would not grow. Phosphate helps with fruit develop and the growth of the plant's roots.
12.) The subsoil is made up of clay. This allows it to store water. A plant's roots will begin in the topsoil, but will need to grow into the subsoil to get access to stored water.
13.) If you dug 3 miles down into the ground, you would hit the bedrock layer. This is the layer that is solid rock. It is often called the parent layer because as the rock within the bedrock layer erodes, they are pushed upward to form new soil.
14.) The subsoil erodes or gets washed away very quickly. To prevent this it has to be covered by the topsoil.
15.) A mudslide can occur when the soil erodes or is washed away over time. This is very dangerous and can lead to homes being damaged.
16.) From the soil we can get things to make medicines, clothing, and use soil for buildings.
17.) False. The tropical rainforest's topsoil is low in nutrients. This is because of the high rainfall. With each rain more and more of the topsoil and its nutrients gets washed away.
18.) Framers can keep the topsoil healthy by rotating crops. Rotating crops helps to keep the nutrient levels high since different crops use different amounts of nutrients to grow and develop.
19.) Exposure to the wind or rainfall causes soil erosion.
20.) Plants need the soil the most. However, animals (including humans) depend on plants for lots of things. Without soil, there would be no plant life, but without plants, there would also be no animal life. All organisms are interconnected in this way.

Earth Science #3: Environmental or Natural Resources

Let's start to put all the pieces of what you have learned together. There are lots of things we get from the environment, we'll review them now.

Rocks – You learned that rocks help to form the soil for plants. Rocks are also important in providing shelter for animals. Think about all the animals that may live on the side of a mountain or inside of a cave. Rocks also store minerals like calcium and phosphorus which are needed by plants and animals to grow and develop.

Earlier, we talked about precious stones. What do you think they are used for? Precious stones like diamonds, rubies, emeralds, and even opal are used for jewelry. This has been a practice for thousands of years. Even the Ancient Egyptians used precious stones for jewelry and to signify royalty and wealth.

Rocks have been used to make weapons or tools. Native Americans would use obsidian, a type of igneous rock to make arrow heads for hunting or for war weapons. The early cavemen would sharpen stones to make simple tools to hit or cut other objects.

Today, we use rocks for buildings, to make strong foundations. Rocks can also be used for decorative purposes like in a garden or for a backyard patio or walkway. Sculptors often use stone to carve figures out of or make statues. Take for example, Mount Rushmore. This is an elaborate stone carving on the side of a mountain with the faces of four famous presidents. The neat thing about stone or rock carvings is that they can last for hundreds of years before they erode. This wouldn't be true with paper or a painting, which would easily get damaged during a rainstorm or in the intense summer heat.

Water – Is the most important substance on Earth. Without water, life would not exist. So what exactly does what help with? Water is an essential part of:

- Temperature regulation: What happens if you are very hot? You sweat! Your body has pores in your skin to release water to help cool you off. Because water is such a strong substance, when it evaporates (goes from liquid to gas), it takes a lot of your body heat with it, leaving you feeling cooler. Did you know water helps to regulate the temperature of the ocean? Yes, it does! In the winter, ice freezes and floats to the ocean's surface. This layer of ice helps to block some of the cold air from getting into the ocean. This leaves the ocean water slightly warmer than the ocean's surface. This does not mean that it is very hot, but is slightly warmer, warm enough for fish, whales, penguins, and other aquatic animals to live through the harsh winter. When the Spring emerges and the temperatures increase, the layer of ice is the first to melt. As the heats up and melts, the liquid water from the melting goes down into the ocean and the ocean water rotates, bringing nutrients from the ocean's surface to the bottom of the ocean.

- Nutrient Transport: Water is what we call the universal solvent. What does that mean? It means that water can dissolve most things. Water cannot dissolve everything, but it can does a lot of important things that our bodies need dissolved. Think about it this way…if water could not dissolve other substances, then we would be unable to move nutrients around our bodies in our bloodstream. Water also helps plants move nutrients throughout the plant's stem and leaves.

- Chemical Reactions: Water is a necessary substance in important chemical reactions that take place in nature. Without water the reactions would not take place at all or be very slow. For example, plants need water to make their own food. The energy from water is combined with the energy from the sunlight to help plants make a special sugar called glucose. This glucose is what the plants needs and uses to survive.

Plants – Plants help other organisms stay healthy. Plants make their own food with sunlight, water, and carbon dioxide (a special gas in the air). Plants are one of the only organisms that can do this. Other organisms like animals have to eat other organisms to get energy. Let's look at the food chain (on the right) to better understand the importance of plants in the ecosystem.

A food chain shows how animals are eaten. The arrow indicates who eats what animal. For example the frog is eaten by the snake and the insect is eaten by the frog. The plant is at the bottom of the food chain. This means that without plants, there would be nothing for the insect to eat. What do you think would eventually happen? The insect would either move to another habitat or die out from starvation. But, then how would that affect the frog? The frog would not have anything to eat if there are not enough insects. So, the frogs may die out. But, then what would happen to the snakes? The snakes would die out and then the eagle would have no food to eat. As you can see, the plant is the foundation or holds up the food chain. Without plants, the other animals would suffer and could die.

We often say that plants are the primary producers. This means that they are the first food source in an ecosystem. We get lots of food from plants like corn, wheat, fruits, nuts, even maple syrup.

Plants are also important in textiles or clothing, building, and in medicine.

If you think of bamboo or an oak tree, they can be used to build homes and they were, and still are, an important building source for hundreds of years. Where do you think rubber comes from? It actually comes from a tree! The rubber tree produces rubber that we use to make plastics of all sorts.

We get cotton from the cotton plant. The cotton can then be woven to make fabrics and the fabrics can be used for various items inside and outside of the home.

Did you know that many plants are herbs that can be used as natural ways to cure illness? The daffodil is used to treat Alzheimer's and the Foxglove plant has been used since the 1500s to treat heart disease.

Not only do plants provide us with food and materials, but they also serve as homes or habitats for thousands of animals. Squirrels, birds, even some snakes live in trees and rely on the tree for shade and shelter from predators.

Where does the oxygen we breathe come from? This comes from plants and trees also! When plants make their own food through a process called photosynthesis, they release oxygen. This is the only way that oxygen is made. If we were to cut down all of the trees and plants, then no more oxygen would be made and animals and humans would be unable to survive. Aquatic plants like seaweed also release oxygen into the oceans for animals like fish and dolphins to breathe. As plants make their own food they use up carbon dioxide. Carbon dioxide is a gas that we release when we breathe out or exhale. It is also released by factories and cars. The only way it can be removed is through photosynthesis. Reducing the levels of carbon dioxide in the air is a good thing for the environment. This helps to reduce the greenhouse effect which is causing the Earth to warm quicker than it should. Plants and animals need each other. Plants need carbon dioxide from animals and animals need the oxygen that the plants make.

Soil – Why is dirt important? Well, dirt or soil as you learned contains nutrients that plants need to grow. Without soil, plants would die out and we discussed the consequences that could have on other animals. Soil can also be a great storage system not just for nutrients but also for water.

Soil also supports life, literally. If we didn't have dirt, we would fall into the hot mantle of the Earth. The soil underneath our homes, schools, and buildings helps to keep them upright.

Soil for hundreds of years has been used as a simple and cheap building material. Clay bricks or mud bricks can be made to create shacks. Mud has been used to create adobe homes or patch up spaces in between wood or brick structures.

You can probably think of at least 5 animals that live in the soil. Where would they live without the soil? For slimy organisms like the earthworm, the soil is the best environment for them since it is dark and damp.

Technology may provide us with lots of other things we need in our lives, but don't forget the natural resources you have around you. Trees may provide you with apples for an apple pie or oxygen for your morning run. Water is great to quench your thirst and to make sure you stay cool at the beach. Plants are important to help feed other organisms. And, the soil is crucial to allow us to live the way we have for thousands of years.

Activities

Explore more about these natural resources with some exciting hands-on activities.

#1 Building Muddy Bricks

Materials:

- Ice cube tray
- Dirt or sand
- Large mixing bowl
- Water
- Measuring cups

Procedure:

1. Measure about a half a cup of dirt and pour it into the mixing bowl.
2. Measure out about ⅔ cup of water and pour into the mixing bowl.
3. Mix the dirt and water together in the bowl.
4. Place the mud into the ice cube openings in the ice cube tray.
5. Let the mud dry for an hour.
6. Then start building!

What's happening?

When dirt is mixed with water it forms mud. Mud has been used for years to build houses or patch up openings between bricks. When the mud is made, it is easy to work with, but when it hardens it forms a brick that can be used to build things.

#2: Filter away!

Materials:

- Water

- 4 different types of soil (can be potting soil, sand, clay, and dirt)

- Filter paper

- Plastic funnel

- 9 Large clear plastic cups

- Cup holder with stand

- Food coloring (red, blue, yellow, and green)

- Knife or scissors (ask for adult help when using these)

Procedure:

1. With an adult's help, poke at least ten holes in each of the plastic cups.

2. Cut out a circular piece of filter paper.

3. Place the circular filter paper in the bottom of each cup.

4. Fill each cup about halfway with soil. One soil type per cup.

5. Sit each cup inside of the plastic funnel with the bottom of the cup resting inside of the funnel.

6. Place each cup into the cup holder and place an empty plastic cup underneath each. This cup will catch the water as it is filtered by the soil.

7. In a separate cup add about 3 cups of water and 5-10 drops of food coloring.

8. Pour the about ¾ of a cup of water solution into each of the cups with soil.

9. Let the water drain out of each cup for 30 minutes.

10. Observe the color of the water collected in each plastic cup. What does the water look like now?

11. Repeat steps 6 - 9 with different colored water mixtures.

What's happening?

Soil is a natural filter. There are small holes in the soil for water to move through, but some things get absorbed. The food coloring gets absorbed in the soil and the water that is collected may have changed colors. In some cases, the water changed colors as it interacted with the components in the soil.

#3: Quick, quick, quick!

Materials:

- Sugar (can be cubes or granulated)

- 2 clear glass cup

- Water (preferably cold water)

- Hot water

- Mixing spoon

- Tablespoon

Procedure:

1. Fill each glass cup with water. One should have cold water and another should have hot water. The cups should have an equal amount of water in each.

2. Place two tablespoons of sugar in the cold water and stir.

3. Repeat step 2 with the hot water. Which glass dissolved the sugar the fastest?

4. Continue to add one tablespoon of water to each mixture, slowly, and stirring each time. Which mixture took more sugar?

What's happening?

Both the cold water and the hot water dissolved the sugar, but one dissolved more. The hot water dissolves more sugar because the water particles are moving faster in the hot water and able to dissolve more than in the cold water. Think about this in nature. The oceans are able to dissolve more nutrients for the animals in the summertime than in the winter when the water is colder.

#4: Water's on the move!

Materials:

- 2 clear plastic cups

- Water

- 3 sheets of paper towel

Procedure:

1. Take the three sheets of paper towel and twist them to make a "paper towel rope".

2. Pour water in one of the plastic cups and sit the two cups side by side.

3. In the cup with water, put one end of the paper towel and drape the other end of the paper towel into the empty plastic cup. So, one end of the paper towel should be in the water and the other end should be in the empty cup without water.

4. Observe the cups for 30 minutes. What happens to the empty cup?

What's happening?

What is a fantastic substance! You may have noticed that the empty cup begin to fill with water. Cool, right? This is called capillary action, where water is able to "walk up" substances to go from one place to another. This is a great way for plants to transport water as it is absorbed in their roots and has to go up through the stem to the leaves.

#5: Colorful dying plants

Materials:

- 10-15 pieces of onion skins
- Large cooking pot
- Water
- Several large raw eggs
- Mixing spoon
- Cloth cut into squares (these should be large enough to wrap the eggs
- Rubber bands

Procedure:

1. Soak the cloth and the onion skin in lukewarm water.
2. Wrap the egg with onion skins until the egg is completely covered.
3. Place the egg inside of the cloth and close shut with the rubber band
4. Fill the cooking pot halfway with water and place the cloth-wrapped eggs into the pot.
5. Ask an adult to place the pot on the stove and boil the eggs for 20-30 minutes.
6. Let the pot cool for 30 minutes and remove the clothed-wrapped eggs.
7. Take off the rubber bands and look at your new dyed eggs!

What's happening?

Plants have special pigments within them that help them to absorb light so that they can go through photosynthesis to make their own food. These same pigments contain colors or dyes that can be used to die cloths or like what you saw eggs! Plants have been used for hundreds if years to make beautiful colors for fabrics and textiles.

Quiz

1. Name two things that rocks provide.
2. Without rocks, there would be no _____.
3. What are precious stones used for?
4. The Native Americans used obsidian to make _____.
5. Why do sculptors use rock instead of other materials like paper?
6. What is the most important substance on Earth?
7. True or False. Water is not involved in temperature regulation (like keeping you cool).
8. True or False. When water freezes, it sinks to the bottom of the ocean.
9. What is the importance of ice?
10. Water is needed to transport _____.
11. What do plants produce that humans and other animals need to survive?
12. True or False. In a food chain, plants are at the top.
13. True or False. Plants are also called the primary producers.
14. What would happen to the other animals in a food chain, if plants were eliminated?
15. Name three things we get from plants.
16. True or False. Maple syrup and rubber come from trees.
17. Name an herb and what it helps to cure.
18. Name two animals that have plant habitats.
19. Name one animal that has soil habitats.
20. Rocks, water, plants, and soil are all considered _____ resources.

Quiz Answers

1. Rocks can provide shelter, soil, art materials, and tools.
2. Without rocks, there would be no soil. Remember soil comes from sediment (or broken rock) mixed with dead matter like leaves and decaying/dead animals.
3. Precious stones are often used to make jewelry.
4. The Native Americans used obsidian to make arrowheads.
5. Sculptors use rock instead of other materials because rock will not fall apart easily. It will eventually erode but only after hundreds of years.
6. Water is the most important substance on Earth. All organisms need water to survive.
7. False. Water is involved in temperature regulation. Think about when you sweat. As you sweat, water leaves your body and evaporates. When it evaporates it takes the heat away from your body and helps you stay cool.
8. False. When water freezes, it rises or floats to the top of the ocean. This is very important because if ice sunk, the oceans may completely freeze, killing all the animals in the ocean.
9. Ice floats and in the winter the layer of ice that forms at the tops of oceans is able to insulate (warm) the water below it.
10. Water is needed to transport nutrients. This is true because water is the universal solvent, meaning it is able to dissolve most substances.
11. Plants produce oxygen which humans and other animals need to survive.
12. False. In a food chain, plants are at the bottom. This does not mean they are unimportant, instead the position at the bottom shows that they support or hold up the other organisms in the food chain.
13. True. Plants are also called the primary producers. This is because they are the first organisms in a food chain. They produce their own food and then are consumed or eaten by other animals in the food chain.
14. Without plants, the other animals would eventually die.
15. From plants we are able to get materials for clothing (cotton), food, oxygen to breathe, medicines, and building materials (wood or bamboo).
16. True. Maple syrup and rubber come from trees.
17. The daffodil is used to treat Alzheimer's and the Foxglove plant has been used since the 1500s to treat heart disease.
18. Answers may vary. In the section, the birds, squirrels, and snakes were given as examples of organisms that live in trees.
19. Answers may vary. In the section, the earthworm was named as an example of an organism that lives in the soil.
20. Rocks, water, plants, and soil are all considered environmental (or natural) resources.

Earth Science #4: Fossils

Fossils are a way that we can learn more about the past. Paleontologists study fossils and the types of life forms that existed millions of years ago. For some organisms that are extinct, like dinosaurs, fossils are the only way we can study them.

What are fossils? How are they formed?

Fossils are the remains of animals and plants and they have been found all over Earth. In order to form a fossil, the animal or plant has to be quickly buried immediately after death. This can be done by sinking into the mud, or being buried by a large sandstorm. Most of the animal will rot or decay, like the fur, skin, organs, and muscles. The harder parts of the animal like the bones and teeth will remain and will be covered with newly formed rock. It is important for the new layer of rock to form quickly so that the animal's remains are not washed away.

Eventually the chemicals that are released by the animals decaying body will cause the bones to remain hard materials of the animal to decompose. As the bone breaks down, minerals come in from the surrounding rock and form a rock impression where the existing bone was. This is what gives the fossil its shape, looking identical to the dead organism.

Material like trees can also form fossils through a process called petrification. In this process, hard and soft portions of a plant or animal are replaced with a special type of natural material called silica or calcite. This causes the wood to look more like rock.

Insects and pieces of plants can get trapped in tree sap and be petrified for millions of years. The tree sap is very sticky but over time can harden and form amber. This is a useful way to study the insects since it keeps them suspend in the amber and their body and parts stay together.

Not all organisms are able to form fossils. Most animals and plants that die decompose, or their remains are washed away. Only a very small percentage of organisms are captured in fossils. Scientists believe that less than 0.1% of all dinosaurs that once roamed the Earth are found in fossils.

What are the different types of fossils?

Each fossil is not created equal. In fact, there are five different types of fossils. They are: cast fossils, mold fossils, carbon film fossils, trace fossils, and preserved remains fossils. We'll look at each type, how their made, and what we can learn from them.

Cast Fossils

If you think of when you have heard the word "cast". If you have ever broken a bone, you may have had to wear a cast to cover the area. Similar to a cast you may have to wear, a cast fossil is a 3-D fossil. It is made by using a mold. A mold is formed when an animal or plant dies lands on rock or a soft material like clay or mud and remains there as it decays. The animal or plant leaves behind a mold or an impression. Over time, water, sediment, and other dissolved minerals like calcium come in and fill the mold. The sediment and minerals begin to come together and form rock, making a cast, or a 3-D image of the animal or plant. As we go on to the next type of fossil, the mold fossil, keep in mind that cast and mold fossils are opposite of each other. In other words, a cast is the opposite of a mold and a mold is the opposite of a cast.

Mold Fossils

If a cast is a 3-D version of the animal, then what is a mold? A mold only forms with animal remains. This is because the hard parts of the animal like the bones will get buried in sand or clay. Over time as the hard parts decay and dissolve they will leave behind an impression of the animal's shape. This is the mold. Mold fossils can sometimes be called impression fossils. Imagine taking a fork and pressing it into a piece of clay. What is left behind are the marks of the fork. This is similar to what happens when a mold fossil is formed. Mold fossils can provide some information about the animal, but because they are only formed from the hard parts of the animal, we do not learn as much as we could.

Carbon Film Fossils

Did you know that all living things have carbon within them? Yes, it is true. Carbon is considered to be one of the first elements on Earth and is within all of us. When an animal or plant dies and is immediately buried in sand, clay, or mud the carbon and other things within them begins to decompose. Over a long period of time, only the carbon will be left. Carbon takes a very long time to disappear. Scientists can study the leftover carbon and learn a little about the soft parts of the animal like the muscles, skin, and even the organs. Carbon film fossils can also be used to study plants and learn more about all parts of the plant including the plant's stem, roots, and leaves.

Trace Fossils

Have you ever left a footprint in the sand or the mud? If so, then you've left a trace fossil. Trace fossils can provide scientists with information about an organism's activities, how they traveled, how heavy they were, etc. The depth and size of the marking left has lots of information that scientists can study. But how does a footprint become a fossil? Eventually the footprint gets buried with layers of sediment and this sediment then turns into solid rock. The rock that results has the same shape and size as the footprint it covered.

Preserved Remains Fossils:

These fossils form when an animal or plant becomes trapped within a substance. Preserved fossils are commonly made from: amber, tar, or ice.

Amber, we talked about, is the solid form of sap from a tree. Insects can get stuck and die and are preserved for thousands, if not millions of years.

When an animal dies and is trapped in a tar pit, the tar eventually soaks into their body and stops the bones from breaking down. This preserves the hard parts of the animal for scientists to study.

Animals that lived in very cold environments may die and become frozen or enclosed in ice. They will stay frozen in the ice for millions of years and scientists can study lots about these animals. Ice keeps the organism intact and scientists can even study the hairs and nails of the animal thousands of years later!

How are fossils found?

Fossils have to be excavated or dug up from rock layers. Sedimentary rocks contain fossils. This is because when an animal or plant dies, it lies on top of a layer of sedimentary rock and is over time covered with the next layer of sedimentary rock. The layers of rock serve to encase or protect the decomposing plant or animal, leaving impressions of the animal or plant in the layers of rock above and below it. Fossils do not contain bones, but do keep their original shape. Since fossils are enclosed in rocks for thousands, if not millions of years, they have more characteristics in common with rocks.

How are fossils dated?

Scientists can use a technique called carbon dating. We know that all organisms have carbon within them and carbon takes about 5,500 years to decompose half of the carbon in an organism. Scientists have samples of very old organisms that they know the age of. When a fossil is found, they can compare the amount of carbon in the fossil to the samples and determine the age of the fossil. The less carbon in the fossil, the older it is. Remember carbon decays very slowly so if only a very small amount is left that means the fossil must have been created thousands, if not millions of years ago for there to be such small amounts of carbon remaining.

Fossils are our view into the past. Through the discovery and study of fossils over 1,000 dinosaurs have been found. The more fossils that are excavated the more we can learn about dinosaurs and other plants and animals. Finding fossils is not a new phenomenon. Many believe that even the Greeks and the Romans discovered and studied fossils hundreds of years ago. There are many more fossils still trapped under layers of rock and Earth that have yet to be discovered. We are even creating fossils today that scientist hundreds and thousands of years from now can study to learn more about our present day plant and animals.

Want to explore more with fossils? Try these hands-on science experiments and keep adding to your knowledge and understanding of fossils! As you work through these experiments test yourself and see if you can keep track of the different types of fossils that were discussed in this section.

Activities

#1: Ready, Set, Cast!

Materials:

- ¥Modeling clay and Plaster of Paris

- ¥plastic soda bottles

- ¥Plastic small toy dinosaurs (or sticks and leaves)

- ¥Large mixing bowl

Procedure:

- 1.   Cut the plastic bottles into two-inch circles or rings.

- 2.   Section off the clay into pieces that can easily fit into the plastic bottle rings, leaving ½ inch space at the top of the ring.

- 3.   Smooth out the clay as much as possible.

- 4.   Take the toy dinosaurs or other objects and press them into the clay for 30 seconds and then remove.

- 5.   Mix the Plaster of Paris in the large mixing bowl. Only mix enough to pour into the plastic ring with the clay.

- 6.   Pour the Plaster of Paris into the rings with the clay, filling it to the top of the ring.

- 7.   Leave the plastic ring with the Plaster of Paris untouched for 30-45 minutes for it to completely harden.

- 8.   Push the clay and the Plaster of Paris out of the ring.

What's happening?

In this experiment, you created a cast fossil. Cast fossils are made when an animal gets trapped in the soil or clay immediately after it dies and then they are covered with sedimentary rock. As the animal decays, the rock replaces the soft and hard parts of the animal's body, leaving a cast. The newly formed rock will take the shape of the animal.

#2: Make a good impression…

Materials:

- ¥Plaster of Paris

- ¥Paper cups (6 ounce size is best)

- ¥Plastic small toy dinosaurs (or sticks and leaves)

- ¥Large mixing bowl

- ¥Napkins or paper towels

Procedure:

- 1.   Cut the tops off of the small paper cups, leaving about one inch of cup.

- 2.   Mix the Plaster of Paris in the large mixing bowl.

- 3.   Pour the Plaster of Paris into the paper cup sections.

- 4.   Let the Plaster of Paris sit for three minutes, allowing it to slowly harden.

- 5.   Take the two dinosaurs or other object and firmly press it into the Plaster of Paris. Be sure not to twist or turn the object. Press firmly down, and let the object remain in the Plaster of Paris for 5 minutes.

- 6.   Slowly and carefully remove the object from the cup.

- 7.   Leave the cup with the Plaster of Paris untouched for 30-45 minutes for it to completely harden.

- 8.   Peel the cup from around the Plaster of Paris.

What's happening?

You've just made a mold fossil. Mold fossils occur when the animal's remains fall on newly formed rock and make an impression in the rock. The other kind of fossil is a cast fossil. Mold fossils provide a 2-D representation of the animal and do not provide as much information as a cast fossil. Fossils of any kind do give scientists an inside view into the life of prehistoric plants and animals.

#3: The bouncy, bouncy egg

Materials:

- ¥Vinegar
- ¥Clear glass jar with lid
- ¥Raw egg

Procedure:

- 1. Fill the glass jar with vinegar within an inch of the top of the jar.
- 2. Carefully place the egg in the jar.
- 3. Put the lid on the glass jar.
- 4. Leave the egg in the jar for at least 4 days, until the shell has disappeared.
- 5. Gently pour out the vinegar.
- 6. Feel the egg, gently squeezing it.

What's happening?

The egg's shell disappeared! The egg's shell is made up of calcium like our bones. When an animal dies they slowly decompose. The soft parts like the organs, skin, and muscles degrade first. Eventually the bones and harder portions of the animal also degrade leaving behind nothing or a fossil if the animal has decomposed on rock. The vinegar is able to eat through the egg's shell, leaving the soft lining of the egg. If you were to leave the egg for weeks, it would completely decompose, leaving no trace of the egg.

#4: Digging for fossils

Note: This experiment requires **adult supervision**.

Materials:

- ¥Chocolate chips (at least 3 cups)

- ¥Metal mixing spoon

- ¥Microwave or cooking pot with stove

- ¥Styrofoam or paper cups

- ¥Gummy worms

- ¥Refrigerator

Procedure:

- 1.   Melt 2 cups of chocolate using the microwave or a cooking pot. Make sure to stir the chocolate every 30-40 seconds to prevent burning. Be very careful handling this as the chocolate will be very hot and can cause burns.

- 2.   Slowly and carefully pour the chocolate into the paper cups. Fill the paper cup about halfway.

- 3.   Place the gummy worm in the chocolate.

- 4.   Fill the rest of the cup with chocolate completely covering the gummy worm.

- 5.   Place the paper cup in the refrigerator for 45-60 minutes.

- 6.   Peel the paper cup from around the chocolate and dig for your gummy worm!

What's happening?

Remember sedimentary rock forms fossils. When an animal dies and falls on already formed rock, new rock forms on top of the animal, encasing it in two layers of rock. This is what you did with your gummy worm. The old rock was the chocolate you poured into the cup in the beginning, and the new rock was the chocolate you poured over the gummy worm. The worm was encased or completely covered with chocolate like an animal is completely covered by rock when a fossil forms.

#5: Under great pressure...

Materials:

- ¥3 slices of bread

- ¥Gummy worms or gummy bears

- ¥Three to four heavy books

- ¥Paper towels

Procedure:

- 1.   Place one slice of bread on a paper towel.

- 2.   Place a few gummy worms/bears on top of the bread.

- 3.   Place another slice of bread and more gummy worms/bears on that layer.

- 4.   Place the final layer of bread on the top.

- 5.   Wrap the entire bread "structure" in a paper towel.

- 6.   Place the paper towel with the bread on top of a book and place several books on top of it.

- 7.   Press firmly down on the top books for 2 minutes.

- 8.   Leave the books on top of the paper towel overnight.

- 9.   Remove the books and open the paper towel to examine the bread and gummy worms.

What's happening?

Fossils are created over time and under lots and lots of pressure. What did the bread mixture look like after it had been under the pressure of the books for several hours? When a fossil forms, the animal's remains are also crushed under the layers of new rock that form.

Quiz

1.) Who studies rocks?

2.) What can we learn from fossils?

3.) True or False. Most organisms form fossils.

4.) How is petrified wood made?

5.) Hardened tree sap is called _____.

6.) How are fossils made?

7.) True or False. Fossils can only be found in the desert.

8.) True or False. Fossils will have the bones of the animal.

9.) Fossils have to be _____.

10.) What type of rock makes fossils?

11.) How are fossils dated?

12.) What are the five types of fossils?

13.) True or False. Scientists can learn more from carbon film fossils than from preserved remains.

14.) Name two types of substances that can create preserved remain fossils.

15.) What is the difference between a cast fossil and a mold fossil?

16.) All organisms have _____ within them.

17.) True or False. Mold fossils are the same as cast fossils.

18.) A footprint is an example of a _____ fossil.

19.) In which type of fossil can the hairs and nails of the organism be studied?

20.) Why would a plant mold fossil not exist?

Quiz Answers

1.)   Paleontologists study fossils.

2.)   Fossils give us a look into the past. They are very helpful in studying plants and animals that are extinct.

3.)   False. Most organisms do not form fossils. Instead, when they die, they are decomposed and their remains are washed away.

4.)   Petrified wood is made when minerals seep into the cracks of the wood and replace most of the wood material with rock.

5.)   Hardened tree sap is called amber. Tree sap is very sticky and can cover an insect and keep it persevered for thousands of years.

6.)   Fossils are made when an organism dies and is immediately covered by rock. The rock layers (above and below) keep the organism in place. As the hard material like bone decomposes over hundreds of years, it leaves an impression behind in the fossil.

7.)   False. Fossils have been found all over the world, on each continent.

8.)   False. Fossils will have the same shape of the animal, but there will be no bone material remaining.

9.)   Fossils have to be excavated or dug up. They are often buried under several layers of rock.

10.)   Sedimentary rocks make fossils.

11.)   Fossils can be dated using a process called carbon dating. Scientists compare the amount of carbon in the fossil with the amount of carbon in other fossils to see how old the fossil is.

12.)   The five types of fossils are: cast fossils, mold fossils, carbon film fossils, trace fossils, and preserved remains fossils.

13.)   False. Scientists can learn more from carbon film fossils than from preserved remains. Preserved remains fossils have the animal intact and allow scientist to study the entire animal. Carbon film fossils are only able to study the animal based on the carbon that remains. Most of the animal would have decomposed by the time scientists find the fossil.

14.)   Preserved remains fossils can be made using amber, tar, or ice.

15.)   A cast fossil is a 3-D representation of the animal whereas a mold fossil is just a 2-D version similar to just an impression fossil.

16.)   All organisms have carbon within them.

17.)   False. Mold fossils are the opposite of cast fossils.

18.)   A footprint is an example of a trace fossil.

19.)   In a preserved remains fossil encased in ice the hairs and nails of the organism can be studied thousands of years later.

20.)   Mold fossils are made from the hard parts of an organism, like the bones. Plants do not have bones and would not have any hard parts to form a mold fossil.

Second Grade Math
For Home School or Extra Practice

By Greg Sherman

Number Sense

One of the first skills we develop as children is counting. Everyone enjoys asking toddlers how old they are and how many fingers they can count. We are constantly counting things, adding and subtracting items, multiplying and dividing quantities during our average day. During third grade, students will learn several new skills with numbers. Some of these skills include how to name numbers, where to position numbers to perform various operations, and specific traits of special numbers, like even and odd numbers.

Numbers from one and higher are classified as Whole Numbers. Zero is an important number, but functions mainly as a placeholder. Numbers between zero and one are composed of fractions and because they have values less than one, they are not defined as Whole Numbers.

To be able to work with Whole Numbers, the students need to learn how to name them based on how many "places" are occupied. For example, the number ten (10) is named as such because it has numbers occupying the ones and the tens places. The table below shows the place values and basic names for Whole Numbers up to One Hundred Thousand:

Ones	Tens	Hundreds	Thousands
1	10	100	1,000

Naming Numbers

Writing Names are given according to the number of "places" the number occupies. For example, 10 is named "ten" because the biggest place it occupies is the tens place.

- One Hundred (100) is named because it occupies up to the hundreds place.
- Two Hundred is named for the number two (2) and the number of places the whole number occupies (200).

- Five Thousand is named for the number five (5) and the number of places the whole number occupies (5,000).

To make naming numbers more interesting, the following examples include numbers in the various places instead of zeros:

- 2,124   Name: Two thousand, one hundred twenty-four
- 357   Name: Three hundred fifty-seven
- 17   Name: Seventeen

When zeros are used as place markers, they are NOT part of the name:

- 102   Name: One hundred two
- 3,052   Name: Three thousand, fifty-five

The above numbers are called Writing Numbers. They are how whole numbers are written when using them in an equation or problem or as a basic description of the number.

Ordinal Names

Another naming process for numbers is using the numbers themselves as place markers. These number names are used for ranking items, ordering number placements in a list, or indicating where numbers are located on a number line relative to each other.

1 2 3 4 5 6 7 8 9 10 11 12 13 14 15 16 17 18 19 20 21 22 23 24 25

The number line above shows whole numbers from One to Twenty-Five. Ordinal naming of the numbers on this number line looks like the following:

FIRST	SECOND	THIRD	FOURTH	FIFTH	SIXTH	SEVENTH	EIGHTH	NINTH	TENTH
1st	2nd	3rd	4th	5th	6th	7th	8th	9th	10h

Using the number line and Ordinal placement names, the following tasks can be performed:

1. What number is the 3rd to the right of 20?

2. If Lisa came in 3rd in the running race, what were the places that came in before?

3. Which number place comes after 36th place?

4. Which place is five places to the left of 14?

Even and Odd Numbers

Even numbers are all multiples of the number two. Or, they are all divisible by two. If a number cannot be divided completely by two (into two equal halves), it is NOT an even number.

Counting by even numbers always results in the next number in line also being even. The following examples are counting using even numbers:

Two's: 2, 4, 6, 8, 10, 12, 14, 16, 18, 20
Four's: 4, 8, 12, 16, 20, 24, 28, 32, 36
Sixes: 6, 12, 18, 24, 30, 36, 42, 48, 54

If a number cannot be completely dived into two equal parts, it is an odd number. In other words, if it is not even, it is odd.

When counting by an odd number, like three, the numbers in the order are presented in a pattern of odd, even, odd, even, etc. The following examples are counting using odd numbers:

Three's: 3, 6, 9, 12, 15, 18, 21, 24, 27, 30

Five's: 5, 10, 15, 20, 25, 30, 35, 40, 45, 50

Seven's: 7, 14, 21, 28, 35, 42, 49, 56, 63, 70

Comparing Numbers

When comparing numbers, students may use a number line or chart to help them understand where each number is in relation to the others. For example, is the number in question greater than or less than another number in the chart or line? When counting by numbers, which number comes next in the order? The best way to visualize how numbers relate to one another is to study a number chart. The one below is up to One Hundred:

1	2	3	4	5	6	7	8	9	10
11	12	13	14	15	16	17	18	19	20
21	22	23	24	25	26	27	28	29	30
31	32	33	34	35	36	37	38	39	40
41	42	43	44	45	46	47	48	49	50
51	52	53	54	55	56	57	58	59	60
61	62	63	64	65	66	67	68	69	70
71	72	73	74	75	76	77	78	79	80
81	82	83	84	85	86	87	88	89	90
91	92	93	94	95	96	97	98	99	100

By using the above chart is becomes easy to answer a few questions:

1. Which number is 5 less than 23?

   By moving 5 numbers back from 23, you get to 18.

2. How many numbers greater is 100 from 84?

   By counting how many numbers are between 84 and 100, you get an answer of 16.

3. If you move 37 places past 22, what number do you land on?

   By counting 37 places past 22, you land on 59.

4. Which number is between 65 and 67?

   By looking at the chart, the student finds 66 is between 65 and 67.

Rounding Numbers

Sometimes to make certain number operations easier for the student, they are first required to "round" the numbers to the simplest amount with regard to place values. The basic rule for rounding up or down is this: if the number is 4 or less you round down, if the number is 5 or greater you round up. The following numbers are examples of "rounding to the nearest tens place value:

Number	Rounded Number to Tens Place	Explanation
14	Round down to 10	14 is closer to 10 than 20
27	Round up to 30	27 is closer to 30 than 20
42	Round down to 40	42 is closer to 40 than 50
57	Round up to 60	57 is closer to 60 than 50

Number Sense – Practice Sheet

1. What is the place value for the number three in 3,526?

2. What is the place value for the number 7 in 743?

3. What is the place value for the zero in 107?

4. Circle the whole numbers: 3, 4.3, 6, ½, 7.1, 9/10

5. True or False: 4 3/4 is a whole number.

Number Names

1. Write the name for 205.

2. Write the name for 1,706.

3. Write the number for Three thousand, fifty-two.

4. Write the name for 47th

5. Write the number for Eighty-Eighth

6. Round 47 to the closest Tens Place

Odds and Evens

1. Is 237 odd or even?

2. Is 425 odd or even?

3. Is 562 odd or even?

4. If you count by three's are all the numbers odd?

5. If you count by four's are all the numbers even?

<u>Comparing Numbers</u>

1. Is 51 greater than or less than 15?

2. Which is the 3rd number after 10?

3. Which five numbers are between 12 and 18?

4. How many zeros are in One Thousand?

5. How many tens (count by tens) are between Twenty and Fifty?

Number Sense - Quiz

1. Write the name for 2,358

2. Write the name for 637

3. Round 84 to the nearest Tens Place:

4. Write the number for Seventy-Ninth

5. Which numbers are in between 23 and 27?

6. Which number is even: 14 or 17

7. Which number is greater: 23 or 32

8. Fill in the missing number: 2   4   _____   8   10

9. If you come in 7th place in a race, how many people came in to the finish before   you?

10. Which number is less than 27:   26 or 28

Addition/Subtraction

During Second Grade, students learn how to add and subtract in a specific order:

- adding and subtracting single-digit numbers
- adding and subtracting double digit numbers
- adding and subtracting triple-digit numbers

Adding and Subtracting Single-Digit Numbers

A quick review of adding single digit numbers:

$1 + 1 = 2$	$2 + 2 = 4$	$3 + 3 = 6$	$4 + 4 = 8$	$5 + 5 = 10$	$6 + 6 = 12$
$1 + 2 = 3$	$2 + 3 = 5$	$3 + 4 = 7$	$4 + 5 = 9$	$5 + 6 = 11$	$6 + 7 = 13$
$1 + 3 = 4$	$2 + 4 = 6$	$3 + 5 = 8$	$4 + 6 = 10$	$5 + 7 = 12$	$6 + 8 = 14$
$1 + 4 = 5$	$2 + 5 = 7$	$3 + 6 = 9$	$4 + 7 = 11$	$5 + 8 = 13$	$6 + 9 = 15$

A quick review of subtracting single-digit numbers:

$2 - 1 = 1$	$4 - 2 = 2$	$6 - 3 = 3$	$8 - 4 = 4$	$10 - 5 = 5$	$12 - 6 = 6$
$3 - 2 = 1$	$5 - 3 = 2$	$7 - 4 = 3$	$9 - 5 = 4$	$11 - 6 = 5$	$13 - 7 = 6$
$4 - 3 = 1$	$6 - 4 = 2$	$8 - 5 = 3$	$10 - 6 = 4$	$12 - 7 = 5$	$14 - 8 = 6$
$5 - 4 = 1$	$7 - 5 = 2$	$9 - 6 = 3$	$11 - 7 = 4$	$13 - 8 = 5$	$15 - 9 = 6$

From adding and subtracting single-digit numbers came the concept and practice of learning *fact families* to help students add and subtract more quickly.

Some Fact Families have been started in the above review of adding and subtracting single-digit numbers:

Example 1

$1 + 2 = 3 \quad 2 + 1 = 3 \quad 3 - 1 = 2 \quad 3 - 2 = 1$

Example 2

$1 + 3 = 4 \quad 3 + 1 = 4 \quad 4 - 1 = 3 \quad 4 - 3 = 1$

Example 3

$1 + 4 = 5 \quad 4 + 1 = 5 \quad 5 - 1 = 4 \quad 5 - 4 = 1$

By memorizing the process of adding two numbers that give the same sum and then when each number is subtracted from that sum it results in the original numbers again, gives the students a pattern they can use to take tests and compute single-digit operations faster.

Basically, it is easier to memorize the relationship between three numbers than trying to memorize each and every individual operation between random numbers.

Adding and Subtracting Double-Digit Numbers

When adding with double-digit numbers, Second Grade students will learn a process called "regrouping." This process was previously taught as "carrying the one" or "carrying the extra or remainder." The other concept the students will learn is to line up the proper place columns. If the numbers being added are not property aligned, the wrong numbers will be added and the student will arrive at an incorrect solution.

Students first begin adding numbers based in ten: 10, 20, 30, 40, etc.

10	20	40	10	30	60	20
+ 20	+ 30	+ 20	+ 10	+ 30	+ 50	+ 50
30	50	60	20	60	110	70

Next, students add double-digit and single-digit numbers without Regrouping:

12	18	23	33	76	47	52
+ 3	+ 1	+ 4	+ 5	+ 2	+ 1	+ 7
15	19	27	38	78	48	59

Adding using Regrouping is then introduced and practiced by the Second Grade students. Regrouping is the process used when the first numbers added produce a double-digit sum. The number in the ones place is written in the sum and the number in the tens place is "regrouped" with the number in the tens place being added.

Example:

$$\begin{array}{r} \text{(regrouped)} \;\; 1 \\ 25 \\ +\;\; 7 \\ \hline 32 \end{array}$$

Since $7 + 5 = 12$, the 2 is placed in the ones place in the sum and the 1 is Regrouped with the 2 in the tens place for 25 giving the correct answer of 32.

The following double-digit addition examples all use Regrouping:

1	1	1	1	1	1	1
27	32	45	85	76	15	57
+ 3	+ 9	+ 6	+ 5	+ 8	+ 9	+ 7
30	41	51	90	84	24	64

1	1	1	1	1	1	1
12	28	23	33	76	47	52
+ 19	+ 13	+ 28	+ 39	+ 36	+ 27	+ 29
31	41	51	72	112	74	81

Subtracting Double-Digit numbers sometimes uses a process called "Borrowing." It is similar in concept to Regrouping, but instead of adding the one to the Regrouped tens place, a value of "10" is moved to the ones place from the tens place of the larger number to allow the subtraction operation to work.

For Example:

$$\begin{array}{r} 25 \\ -\;\; 7 \\ \hline 18 \end{array} \quad\longrightarrow\quad \begin{array}{r} 20 + (5) \\ -\;\; 7 \\ \hline 18 \end{array} \quad\longrightarrow\quad \begin{array}{r} 10 + (15) \\ -\;\; 7 \\ \hline 18 \end{array}$$

The above example shows that since the 5 is too small to subtract 7, the 5 "Borrows" a "10" from the "20" to make 15. The 20 is reduced to a 10 and now the 7 can be subtracted from 15 which gives the answer of 8. The 10 is brought down into the answer to give the correct answer of 18.

As with addition, Borrowing is not always necessary. The following examples show subtraction problems that both need to use Borrowing and those that don't:

27	32	45	85	76	15	57
- 3	- 9	- 6	- 5	- 8	- 9	- 7
24	23	39	80	68	6	50

57	28	83	43	76	47	52
- 19	- 13	- 28	- 39	- 36	- 25	- 39
38	15	55	4	40	23	13

Adding and Subtracting Triple-Digit Numbers

Adding and subtracting triple-digit numbers is essentially the same as adding and subtracting double-digit numbers with respect to Regrouping and Borrowing, but it sometimes needs an extra step to complete the process.

Borrowing, for example, requires an extra step:

$$
\begin{array}{r} 251 \\ - \ 67 \\ \hline 184 \end{array}
\quad\longrightarrow\quad
\begin{array}{r} 200 + 50 + 1 \\ - \ 67 \\ \hline 184 \end{array}
\quad\longrightarrow\quad
\begin{array}{r} 100 + 140 + 11 \\ - \ 60 + \ 7 \\ \hline 184 \end{array}
$$

The above example shows that since the 1 is too small to subtract 7, the 1 "Borrows" a "10" from the "50" to make 11. The 50 is reduced to a 40 and now the 7 can be subtracted from 11 which gives the answer of 4. Now, 40 is too small to subtract 60, so the 40 Borrows 100 from 200 to make 140. When 60 is subtracted from 140 the answer is 80. The 100 is brought down into the answer to give the correct answer of 184.

Otherwise, the following triple-digit number problems are just like single-digit and double-digit number problems:

327	532	745	285	177	619	757	984
+ 4	+ 7	+ 3	+ 5	- 8	- 9	- 4	- 7
331	539	748	290	169	610	753	977

157	328	183	343	576	647	852	943
+ 19	+ 13	+ 28	+ 39	- 15	- 25	- 41	- 67
176	341	211	382	561	623	711	876

225	208	873	543	766	497	952	457
+ 129	+ 413	+ 628	+ 137	- 236	- 325	- 839	- 125
354	621	1,501	680	530	172	113	332

When subtracting numbers with zeros, the borrowing begins with the first zero rather than the end of the number as with non-zero numbers.

So, when borrowing to complete this subtraction problem, it starts with the first zero borrowing 100 and then the second zero borrowing 10. Then the problem looks like this:

$$
\begin{array}{r} 200 \\ -\ 125 \\ \hline 75 \end{array}
\quad\longrightarrow\quad
\begin{array}{r} 100 + 90 + 10 \\ -\ 100 + 20\ + 5 \\ \hline 0 + 70\ + 5 \end{array}
$$

205	200	870	503	706	490	900	450
- 129	- 113	- 628	- 137	- 236	- 325	- 839	- 125
76	87	242	366	470	165	61	325

Addition and Subtraction - Practice Sheet

Fill in the missing numbers:

1. $1 + 3 = 4$

    $3 + \_\_\_ = 4$

    $4 - 1 = 3$

    $4 - \_\_\_ = 1$

2. $2 + 5 = 7$

    $\_\_\_ + 2 = 7$

    $7 - \_\_\_ = 2$

    $7 - \_\_\_ = 5$

Solve (remember to line up proper places or columns to get the correct answer)

1. $12 + 1 =$

2. $32 + 84 =$

3. $810 + 21 =$

4. $90 - 12 =$

5. $98 - 15 =$

6. $992 - 827 =$

7. $85 + 95 =$

8. $410 + 127 =$

9. $321 + 620 =$

10. $87 - 18 =$

11. $726 - 552 =$

12. $565 - 221 =$

13. $97 + 12 =$

14. $123 + 456 =$

15. $722 + 32 =$

Greater Than, Less Than, Equal To

1. $12 + 14 + 1$ _____ $30 - 3$

2. $125 - 18$ _____ $100 + 2 + 3$

3. $715 - 113$ _____ $300 + 200 + 157$

Addition and Subtraction - Quiz

Fill In the Blanks

1.   12 + _____ = 17, _____ + 12 = 17, 17 - _____ = 12, 17 – 12 = _____

2.   23 + _____ = 50, _____ + 23 = 50, 50 - _____ = 23, 50 – 23 = _____

Solve

1.   871 + 123 =

2.   726 – 13 =

3.   35 + 27 =

4.   872 – 773 =

5.   73 + 271 =

6. $956 - 897 =$

7. $25 + 29 =$

8. $621 - 599 =$

Fractions

Learning fractions and their functions opens a new world of math and its various uses for the Second Grade student. After learning some of the properties of fractions, students will be able to identify their uses in our daily lives.

When we bake or cook, the measurements are generally in fractions. For example, when baking cookies, the recipe usually calls for one-half cup of sugar, three-quarters cup of brown sugar, one-half cup butter, etc. Many of the tools used to fix cars and other items around the house are calculated in fractions. It is common to find a 3/4 inch wrench or a 5/16 socket in a basic home toolbox.

Fractions are numbers that are less than one, but greater than zero. These numbers all have values between zero and one. Some are very close in value to one like the fraction 9/10. They are equal parts of the Whole Number One.

Fractions are composed of two different numbers. The top number is called the numerator and the bottom number is called the denominator. The numerator represents part of the total and the denominator is the total amount represented.

$$\frac{\text{NUMERATOR}}{\text{DENOMINATOR}}$$

It is easier to see what a fraction really represents by using lists of items and pie charts. These visual tools show what the whole amount looks like and how the fraction covers only a part of the whole.

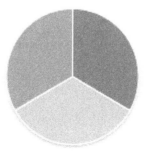

The above picture shows three equal sections of a pie. Since the total number of sections is three, the denominator of the fraction for this picture is 3. The numerator can be 1, 2, or 3 depending on what question is being asked:

1. What is the fraction of the circle colored the lightest gray? 1 out of 3 so, 1/3 is   the fraction.

2. What is the fraction for the lightest section and the darkest sections together? 2 out   of 3 sections are

described, so 2/3 is the fraction.

3. What fraction represents the entire circle? Since there are three sections, and the entire pie is composed of three sections, the fraction is 3/3.

Other examples of visual fraction pictures are presented below:

The total number of squares is 5, so the denominator is 5.

What fraction of 5 is the white square? Since there is only one white square, the fraction is 1 out of 5 or 1/5. AND, if the one white square is 1/5, the 4 remaining black squares are the fraction 4/5.

The total number of triangles is 6, so the denominator is 6.

What are the fractions that represent the number of white triangles out of 6 and the number of black triangles out of 6? There are 2 white triangles, so their fraction is 2/6 and there are 4 black triangles, so their fraction is 4/6.

Equal Halves

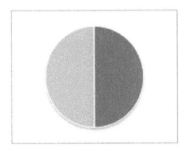 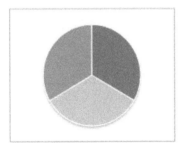 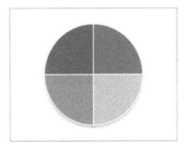

Equal Halves   Equal Thirds   Equal Fourths
(2 parts of 2)   (3 parts of 3)   (4 parts of 4)

The above pies show equal parts of the whole. Each pie is the same size, but can be divided in many different ways and create many different kinds of fractions. One piece of each pie is represented as 1 part of the whole number of pieces. So, one part of two is 1/2, one part of three is 1/3, and one part of four is 1/4.

IT IS VERY IMPORTANT TO REMEMBER that the larger the denominator, the smaller the fraction. For example, as demonstrated by the above pies, 1/4 is smaller than 1/3, which is smaller than 1/2.

Based on the above information, the following comparisons can be made:

1. Greater Than or Less Than: 5/6 > 5/8 > 5/10 AND 3/10 < 3/8 < 3/4 because the larger the denominator, the smaller the individual pieces of the whole.

2.   Equivalent Fractions: Using the pie charts above, which two fractions are equal?   If the charts are compared based on the area covered by the individual pieces of   each chart, it can be seen that two of   the Equal Fourths cover the same area as   one of the Equal Halves. Therefore, 2/4 and 1/2 are equivalent fractions.

3.   Fractions that Equal One:

    If the denominator is the total number of parts in the whole   and the numerator is a   portion of the whole number, then if the numerator and denominator are equal, all   the parts of the total are represented and the fraction equals the whole.

            So, 1 = 2/2 = 3/3 = 4/4 = 5/5 ... 100/100 etc.

The following problems are examples of what Second Grade students will be learning:

1.   Color in 2/5 of the circle below:

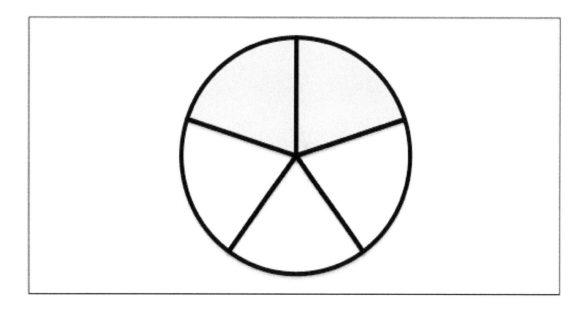

2.   Color in half of the sections (3/6)

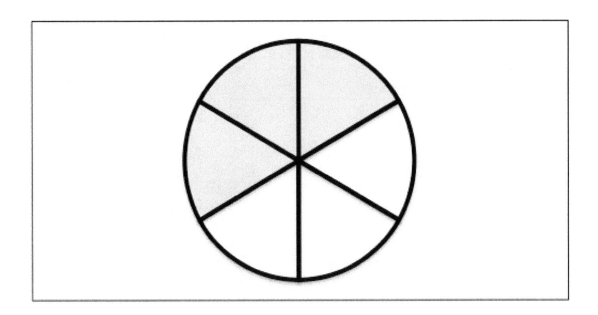

3.

How many lightening bolts are there?   7

How many are shaded?   5

How many are white?   2

What is the fraction of lightening bolts that are shaded?   5/7

What is the fraction of lightening bolts that are white?   2/7

What is the fraction that represents all of the lightening bolts?   7/7 = 1

4.

How many total shapes? 5

How many suns?   3

How many moons?   2

What fraction of the total shapes are the suns?   3/5

What fraction of the shapes are moons?   2/5

5.   Based on the graphs in Questions 1 and 2, which is bigger: 2/5 or 3/6?

Answer: 3/6

6.   Indicate in the following sets of fractions, which are greater than, lesser than, or   equal:

3/3 ___=__ 7/7   3/5 _____>____ 3/8   99/100 _____>___ 98/100

23/25 ____<___24/25   1/2 _____<____2/2   4/4 _____=____8/8

7.   Indicate what fraction the shaded objects represent:

= 3/4   = 5/6

8.

Fill in the blanks

Fill in the blanks

1/2 1/3 1/4 [   ]1/6 1/7 Answer: 1/5

1/8 2/8 3/8 4/8 [   ]   6/8 7/8 8/8 Answer: 5/8

1/1 2/2 [   ] 4/4 5/5 6/6 7/7 Answer: 3/3

9. Which row from number 8 has all the fractions equal to 1? Answer: Row 3

Elementary students will practice and learn fractions throughout their educational experience. Practice solving problems like those presented above, will help students approach learning fractions with more confidence and assurance, which makes fractions appear less complicated and intimidating.

Fractions – Practice Sheet

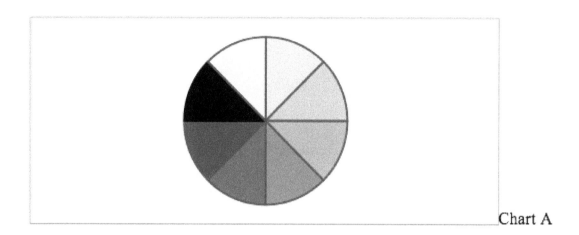

Chart A

1. How many pieces total are there in the above pie chart?

2. If you put the white piece and the darkest piece together what would be the   fraction?

3. How many pieces equal 1/2 of the pie?

4. What is the fraction for just one piece?

5. If you picture the pie chart as a clock face, how many pieces equal 1/4 hour (15   min)?

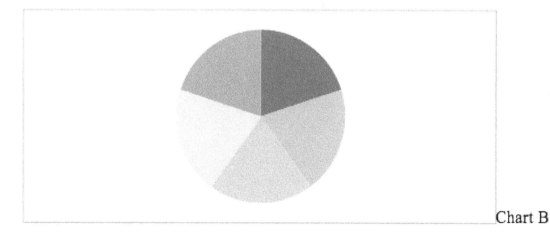

Chart B

6. Is one piece from Chart A bigger or smaller than one piece from Chart B?   [smaller]

7. Which is bigger, 1/8 or 1/5?

Answer the following questions using Chart A and Chart B:

8. Which is bigger, 3/5 or 4/8?

9. If each chart were a real pie, which one would feed more guests?

10. What is the denominator for Chart A? Chart B?

Answer the following questions using the above set of shapes:

1. What is the total number of shapes?

2 How many squares are there?

3. Write the number of squares and the total number of shapes as a fraction:

4. How many shapes are not circles?

5. What fraction of the total shapes are circles?

6. What fraction of the total shapes are triangles?

Compare Fractions

7. Put these fractions in order of smallest to largest:2/3 2/7 2/5

8. Indicate whether the fractions are Greater Than, Less Than, or Equal: 7/7 ___ 3/3

9. Which Numerator is Greater: 5/16 or 9/10

10. Which Denominator is Greater: 1/8 or 4/7

Fractions - Quiz

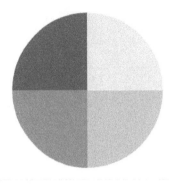

1.   How many pieces are there in the above pie chart?

2.   What fraction is the lightest color?

3.   How many pieces make 1/2 of the pie chart?

4.   What is the fraction for 3 of the four pieces?

5.   What denominator should be used for the above set of lightening bolts?

6.   What is the fraction for the white lightening bolt?

7.   What fraction of the lightening bolts are gray?

8.   What fraction of the lightening bolts are black?

Compare

9. Which is greater: 7/8 or 1/9

10. How many of the fraction 1/16 are needed to make a fraction equal to 1?

Operations

Other than the traditional math operations, like addition and subtraction, other types of math operations will be taught in Second Grade. These operations include, understanding place values, estimating and rounding numbers based on place values, learning time and calendar functions, and the beginnings of multiplication and division.

Number Places

Second Grade students will learn number places up to One Thousand. The number places are as follows:

1s   1, 2, 3, 4, 5, 6, 7, 8, and 9

10s   10, 20, 30, 40, 50, 60, 70, 80, and 90

100s 100, 200, 300, 400, 500, 600, 700, 800, and 900

1000s   1,000   2,000   3,000   4,000   5,000   6,000   7,000   8,000   and   9,000

The various zeros in the 10s, 100s, and 1000s places are replaced with standard numbers to create the whole numbers students will use in their math operations. The following examples show how students will practice and learn place values:

1.   What is the place value for the number 7?

     1,007   ones

     1,271   tens

     1,788   hundreds

     7,102   thousands

2.   Write out the following numbers into their expanded forms

     25   =   20 + 5

     146 =   100 + 40 + 6

2,789   =   2,000 + 700 + 80 + 9

3.   Regroup the following expanded numbers

4 tens + 18 ones   =   5 tens + 8 ones

3 tens + 25 ones   =   5 tens + 5 ones

3 hundreds + 13 tens + 6 ones   =   4 hundreds + 3 tens + 6 ones

8 hundreds + 24 hundreds + 12 ones   = 10 hundreds + 5 hundreds + 2 ones

4.   Convert from expanded numbers to regular numbers

100 + 30 + 5   =   135

20 + 7   =   27

3,000 + 400 + 50 + 9   =   3,459

Time and Calendar Functions

The above clocks are called analog clocks because they do not use digital technology to display the time. Digital clocks display the time exactly as it is written by using numbers to represent the hours and minutes separated by a colon.

For example, the above times written in standard time format (also digital) look like this:

2:00   2:15   2:30   2:45

One piece of information that analog clocks do not display is whether the time is PM (Noon to Midnight) or AM (Midnight to Noon). So, when reading the time from an analog clock, the student will need to have AM or PM information provided in the problem.

Times that occur on the hour, the big hand (minute hand) on the 12 and the little hand (hour hand) on the number can be written with an O'clock descriptor. So, the above 2:00 can also be written as 2 O'clock. PM and AM still need to be added to determine day or night distinctions.

The above times are also learned as fractions of time:

2:15 (AM or PM) = Quarter after Two, Quarter past Two, and 1/4 past the hour

2:30 (AM or PM) = Half (1/2) past Two, Half (1/2) past the Hour

2:45 (AM or PM) = Quarter to Three and 1/4 to Three

Students also learn that there are 24 hours in a day (AM and PM combined) and that although analog clocks are set for standard time, digital clocks and written time can be expressed in military time or by using a 24-hour clock. They will only need to learn Standard Time.

Learning to read and use a calendar are also skills students are taught in Second Grade. Math elements are involved because the standard calendar is divided into days, weeks, and months and each has a numerical value. Students learn that there are seven days in one week and generally thirty days per month. They learn more specifically that certain months have 30 days, some have 31 days, and that February is tricky because is although it usually has 28 days, every four years has 29 days.

If the students are told that the week begins on Sunday and ends on Saturday they can answer some basic calendar questions:

1. Which day of the week is three from Monday?   Thursday

2. How many days are not on the Weekend?   Five

3. How many days are in a week?   Seven

4. Which day is considered to be the middle day?   Wednesday

5. Which day of the week begins with the letter F?   Friday

6 How many days begin with the letter T?   Two

7. What days of the week do you go to school?   Monday, Tuesday, Wednesday, Thursday, and   Friday

Students also learn the order of the 12 months on the calendar:

January
February
March
April
May
June
July
August
September
October
November
December

2013/2014

S	M	T	W	T	F	S
1	2	3	4	5	6	7
8	9	10	11	12	13	14
15	16	17	18	19	20	21
22	23	24	25	26	27	28
29	30	(31)				

Students will be expected to know the following facts about the months of the year:

- January 1 is the first day of each year and is called New Year's Day
- During a Leap Year, February has 29 days instead of 28.
- The year is divided into 4 seasons: Winter, Spring, Summer and Fall.
- The end of each year is December 31 and is called New Year's Eve.

Multiplication and Division

Students will learn multiplication tables up to 10 and be able to divide numbers up to 10. They will first learn how to count groups of numbers:

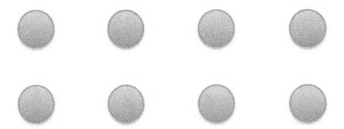

1. How many circles total? 8

2. How many rows of 4 are there?   2

3. If you add 2 rows of 4, how many circles do you have?   8

4. How many columns of 2 are there?   4

5. If you add 4 rows of 2, how many circles do you have?   8

So, if you add 2 together 4 times or you add 4 together 2 times each answer is 8. Therefore, 2 times 4 and 4 times 2 both equal the total number of 8 circles.

Once the Second Grade students have a basic understanding of how multiplication is related to addition, they can begin memorizing their multiplication tables.

Using the above circles again, students can begin learning division:

1. How many circles total? 8

2. How many rows of 4 are there?   2

3. How many columns of 2 are there?   4

So, the total number of 8 circles can be divided into 2 groups of 4 or 4 groups of 2.

Operations – Practice Sheet

Place Values

1. What is the place value of the 8 in 185?

2. What is the place value of the 9 in 19?

3. What is the place value of the 2 in 207?

4. What is the place value of the 4 in 4,123?

Expanded Numbers

1. Write out the expanded number for 352:

2. Write out the expanded number for 85:

3. Write out the expanded number for 1,278:

4. Write the standard number for 20 + 9:

5. Write the standard number for 300 + 70 + 3:

6. Write the standard number for 5,000 + 200 + 20 + 1:

The clock above shows the hour hand on the 2 and the minute hand on the 12. The time represented is 2:00.

1. If it is during the day, is the time 2:00 AM or 2:00 PM?

2. If the minute hand is moved to the 6, is the time 2:15 or 2:30?

3. If the hour hand is moved to the 6, and it is after midnight but before noon, what time is it?

4. If the time is 8:15 PM, is it also 1/4 after 8:00 PM or 1/4 to 8:00 PM?

Calendar

1. Which day of the week begins with the letter W?

2. How many days are in the weekend?

3. Which days are the weekend days?

4. Which day is next after Thursday?

Multiplication and Division

1. If there are 3 groups of 5 apples to be shared, how many people get an apple?

2. If there are 25 pencils and 5 students, how many pencils will each student get?

Operations – Quiz

1. What is the place value of the Zero in 1,027?

2. What is the place value of the 7 in 7,002?

3. Write the standard number for 300 + 2 + 5:

4. Expand the number 7,329:

5. Write an equivalent equation for 3 tens + 26 ones:

6: If the time is 4:15 PM, what number is the hour hand pointing to?

7. If it is Tuesday, what is the name of the day to come next?

8. How many days per week do students go to school?

9. Since January is the first month of the year, what month is 4th ?

10. Fill in the spaces: 5 x _____ = 50 AND 50 ÷ 5 = _____

Money

It is very important to learn about money at an early age. In Second Grade students learn the correct value for each Coin and Bill. The money we earn and spend is referred to as Currency.

The list below contains the common coin and bill amounts that students will be expected to learn:

COINS		BILLS
Penny = 1¢		One Dollar = $1
Nickel = 5 Pennies = 5¢		Five Dollars = $5
Dime = 2 Nickels = 10 Pennies = 10¢		
Quarter = 5 Nickels = 25 Pennies = 25¢		

Dollars and Cents

Recognizing the types of Currency involved in a math problem is the first step to learning other functions involving money. The symbols shown next to the above coin and bill amounts represent dollars ($) and cents (¢). For the amounts below, indicate which are dollars and which are cents:

$5	3¢	7¢	$6	25¢	$17	$100	32¢	18¢	$3
Dollars	Cents	Cents	Dollars	Cents	Dollars	Dollars	Cents	Cents	Dollars

Indicate the type of coin or dollar that is represented below:

AMOUNT	CURRENCY
1¢	Penny
$1	Dollar Bill
5¢	Nickel
$5	Five Dollar Bill
10¢	Dime
25¢	Quarter

Similar to expanded numbers, dollars and cents can be grouped together in many different quantities and arrangements to create the same total amount.

For example, 15¢ can be separated into the following combinations of coins:

1 dime and 1 nickel = 10¢ + 5¢

1 dime and 5 pennies = 10¢ + 1¢ + 1¢ + 1¢ + 1¢ + 1¢

1 nickel and 10 pennies = 5¢ + 1¢ + 1¢ + 1¢ +1¢ + 1¢ + 1¢ + 1¢ + 1¢ + 1¢ + 1¢

Using the above concept create two different combinations of coins for the following amounts:

AMOUNT	COMBINATION 1	COMBINATION 2
30¢	2 dimes and 2 nickels	1 dime, 2 nickels, and 10 pennies
45¢	1 quarter and 2 dimes	4 dimes and 1 nickel
71¢	2 quarters, 2 dimes and 1 penny	1 quarter, 4 dimes, 1 nickel, and 1 penny
84¢	8 dimes and 4 pennies	3 quarters, 1 nickel, and 4 pennies
93¢	3 quarters, 1 dime, 1 nickel, and 3 pennies	9 dimes and 3 pennies

Dollar bills are made from the value from coins. Instead of carrying around hundreds of coins, certain amounts of money were printed on paper notes and used in place of the coins. The following amounts of coins equal one-dollar bill: 4 quarters, 10 dimes, 20 nickels, and 100 pennies. Now, create combinations of bills and coins from the following amounts:

AMOUNT	COMBINATION 1	COMBINATION 2
100¢	2 quarters and 5 dimes	3 quarters, 2 dimes and 1 nickel
137¢	1 dollar bill, 3 dimes, and 7 pennies	1 dollar bill, 1 quarter, 1 dime, and 2 pennies
150¢	1 dollar bill and 2 quarters	4 quarters and 5 dimes

Adding and subtracting monetary amounts is just like adding and subtracting regular numbers. Students will practice adding and subtracting money up to the amount of one dollar similar to the problems below:

17¢	23¢	56¢	12¢	45¢	85¢	99¢	37¢	25¢	74¢
+ 5¢	+ 4¢	+ 13¢	+ 82¢	+ 30¢	- 20¢	- 45¢	- 27¢	- 10¢	- 50¢
22¢	27¢	69¢	94	95¢	65¢	54¢	10¢	15¢	24¢

To better represent how currency is written when dollars bills and coins are combined, the decimal point is used to separate coin amounts from dollar amounts. In addition, the coin amounts only go up to 2 places to the right of the decimal and only up to a total of 99¢. Once the amount of one dollar is reached, the amount is expressed on the left side of the decimal. An example of how dollars and cents are written together is presented below:

Dollars	Cents in amounts of 10¢	Cents in penny amounts (1¢)	Proper written total Amount
2	20	8	$2.28
1	50	7	$1.57
5	80	3	$5.83

As shown above, when dollars and cents are written as combined amount, only the dollar ($) symbol is used. Even if only cents are represented, the dollar sign is used as shown in the following example:50 cents = 50¢ = $0.50

The zero to the left is a placeholder. The zero to the right of the 5 is actually the ones place (pennies) and is needed to complete the number Fifty (50).

The following examples using dollars and cents are written with the decimal point and dollar sign:

NOTE: unlike traditional decimal places, the first place is the tens and the second   place is the ones.

Amount	Written Description	Amount	Written Description
$2.27	Two Dollars and Twenty-Seven Cents	$2.50	Two Dollars and Fifty Cents
$5.56	Five Dollars and Fifty-Six Cents	$1.25	One Dollar and Twenty-Five Cents
$1.75	One Dollar and Seventy-Five Cents	$4.80	Four Dollars and Eighty Cents
$8.32	Eight Dollars and Thirty-Two Cents	$3.90	Three Dollars and Ninety Cents

How many of the above amounts could have pennies included?

Five. The amounts with a number in the ones place ($0.01) are $2.27, $5.56, $1.75, $8.32, and $1.25.

How many of the amounts could have quarters in the cents portion?

All of them could have quarters. Since one quarter = 25 cents = $0.25, and the smallest amount above in the cents portion is $0.25, one or more quarters could be part of the total amount of cents in each money description.

Since exchanging money for goods is something we do every time we buy something, the following examples present situations involving adding and subtracting various amounts of money:

1.   Sara has 3 quarters and 2 dimes (95¢). She wants to buy two candy bars for 20¢   each.   Does she have enough money?   Yes. 95¢ - 40¢ = 55¢

2.   With her change (left over money) can she buy 2 more candy bars?

     Yes. 55¢ - 40¢ = 15¢

3. Based on her change in Question 2, how many nickels does Sara need to get one   more candy bar?

    She needs a total of 20¢ to get another candy bar. She has 15¢, so she needs   1 nickel (5¢) to total 20¢

Money – Practice Sheet

Names and Amounts of Coins

1. Which coin has an amount of 25 cents?

2. Which coin has the amount of 1 cent?

3. What is the value of a dime?

4. What is the value of a nickel?

5. How many quarters in One Dollar?

6. How many dimes in One Dollar?

7. How many pennies in One Dollar?

8. How many nickels in one dime?

9. How many pennies in one dime?

10. How many dimes in one quarter?

Combinations and Amounts

1. How much money is 2 quarters and 3 pennies?

2. How much is 3 dimes, 2 nickels and 4 pennies?

3. How much is 3 quarters and 3 dimes?

4. How much is 2 Dollars and 4 dimes?

5. Which coins would be left if you started with 3 quarters and 3 dimes and spent 2   quarters and 1 dime?

6. If you started with 6 dimes and 3 nickels and spent 2 dimes and 1 nickel, how many quarters could you exchange the remaining dimes and nickels for?

7. If Tim started with $3.89 and bought a book for $1.23, what would he have left?

8. If Joy started with $3.25 and earned $2.00 for walking the dog and $1.00 for   setting the table, how much will she have to go shopping?

9. How much money will Sam have at the end of the week if he earns $8.75 and spends $6.25?

10. If Josie starts with $9.85 and spends $7.38 on school supplies, how much would   she have left?

Money – Quiz

1. How many dimes equal the same amount as 6 quarters?

2. What is the name of the coin that is equal to 5 pennies?

3. How many pennies in One Dollar?

4. How many nickels in 3 quarters?

5. What combination of quarters, dimes, and pennies is $0.98?

6. Write out the currency value for 3 quarters, 4 dimes, and 2 nickels:

7. If Danny earns $3.00 from his aunt, $2.50 from his Grandpa, and $1.25 from his   cousin, what would be the total amount of money Danny earned?

8. If Lisa has 6 quarters and 21 pennies, does she have enough money to buy a slice   of pizza for $1.75?

9. If Lisa borrows $0.20 from her friend Luke, what will her change be after buying   the pizza?

10. How much money will Brian have if he finds 2 quarters, 6 dimes, 4 nickels and 13 pennies?

Shapes/Patterns

Many patterns are found throughout the subject of Second Grade Math. There are repeating patterns, increasing patterns, decreasing patterns, and finally counting patterns.

Patterns are seen all around us. For example, traffic lights present a repeating pattern. They turn green to indicate to drivers that they should move forward through the intersection, second, they turn yellow to warn drivers to slow down because finally, they turn red to alert cars to stop. This pattern is repeated many times daily to prevent accidents within the intersection. An example of an increasing pattern is the scoring used in football games. Each touchdown is 6 points (I am not counting the extra point to keep this simple). So, each time the team scores, their total points increase by 6. Basically, it is counting by sixes.

Repeating Patterns

Before learning how to use counting patterns, Second Grade students learn how to identify patterns by using shapes to represent the items in the pattern. The following examples represent repeating patterns:

1. Based on the above pattern, which picture will be the next in line?   Moon

2. Write in words what this pattern is repeating.

    Answer: star, moon, star, moon, star, moon, star, moon, star

3. If a second moon is added to each current moon, what would the pattern look like?

    Answer: star, moon, moon, star, moon, moon, star, moon, moon, star, moon,   moon,   star

4. What would the pattern be if a sun were added after each moon?

    Star, moon, sun, star, moon, sun, star, moon, sun, star, moon, sun, star

Repeating patterns can involve many different elements. For example, instead of just repeating two single items, the pattern can repeat as many groups of items as you can possibly think of, but that gets a bit complicated for Second Grade Math. Another simple repeating pattern could be using pairs of items, instead of just single items. If that were incorporated into the above pattern concept, it would look like this:

Increasing Patterns

Items that are arranged in an increasing pattern can be very simple up to being quite complicated. Increasing patterns involve adding at least one item to one element of the pattern. More than one item can be added to the element and more than one element in a pattern can be increased. The following pattern only has one element increasing throughout:

1.   Which shape in the pattern is increasing in number?   Square

Many times, a single element will be chosen to be the item that is increased according to a certain formula for the pattern. The above pattern shows that the square is increased by one each time it follows a circle.

2.   Given the pattern, how many squares will be added after the next circle?

Based on the pattern of adding one square to each set of squares after each circle, the next set of squares should have 5 items.

3.   Do the circles change in this pattern?

No. The circles are not part of the increasing element.

Decreasing Pattern

This type of pattern is similar in concept to the increasing pattern, except it is more like a countdown. An element in the pattern begins with a larger quantity and gets smaller as the pattern progresses. The example above with the squares and circles can be turned into a decreasing pattern by going in reverse order. The pattern would then be 4 squares, 1 circle, 3 squares, 1 circle, 2 squares, 1 circle, and finally, 1 square.

Counting and Number Patterns

Using the above examples, determine whether the following number patterns are repeating, increasing, or decreasing:

A. 1 2 1 2 2 1 2 2 2 1 2 2 2 2   Increasing Pattern

B. 3 3 5 5 3 3 5 5 3 3 5 5 3 3   Repeating Pattern

C. 100 99 98 97 96 95 94   Decreasing Pattern

Other Number/Counting patterns include the "skip counting" students learn to help them memorize certain addition and later multiplication problems.

The beginning of "skip counting" usually starts with counting by twos. It will be apparent which type of pattern "skip counting" produces when seen below:

Twos   2 4 6 8 10 12 14 16 18

Threes   3 6 9 12 15 18 21 24 27

Fours   4 8 12 16 20 24 28 32 36

Fives   5 10 15 20 25 30 35 40

As can be seen from the above "skip counting" patterns, they are an increasing type pattern.

Using other types of numbers and number sequences can produce other types of patterns. For example, the pattern below uses even and odd numbers, what type of pattern is it?

3 4 3 4 3 4 3 4 3 4   This produces a Repeating Pattern

5 10 15 20 25 30 35 40   Counting by 5s produces an Increasing Pattern and a
    Repeating Pattern of Odds and Evens

The following examples show how patterns can be created by implementing one or more basic rules for the specific math operation:

1. Add two to every even number when counting by Ones: 1, 4, 3, 6, 5, 8, 7, 10,
            9, 12, 11

2. Count by 3s from 23:   23, 26, 29, 32, 35, 38, 41, 44, 47, 50

3. Count by 5s from 50:   50, 55, 60, 65, 70

Fill in the Missing Numbers

1. 12, 14, ____, 18, 20, 22 The pattern is counting by 2s, so the answer is 16.

2. 40, 50, 60, ____, 80, 90 The pattern is counting by 10s, so the answer is 70.

3. 93, 90, 87, ____, 81, 78 The pattern is decreasing by 3s, so the answer is 84.

What is the next number in the Sequence?

1. 1, 2, 1, 2, 1, 2, 1, ____   The pattern is repeating 1 and 2, so the answer is 2.

2. 3, 1, 1, 4, 1, 1, 5, 1, 1, ____   The pattern is increasing by 1s after two consecutive 1s, so the answer is 6.

3. (1+2), (1+3), (1+4), _____   The pattern is showing adding 1 to a single number in an increasing pattern, so the answer is (1+5).

Shapes/Patterns - Practice Sheet

Define the following types of Patterns

1.

2.

3.

Based on the above patterns, Answer the following questions:

1. What is the next shape in the first pattern?

2. What is the next shape in the second pattern?

3. What is the next shape in the third pattern?

Fill in the Blanks

1. 5, 10, _____, 20, 25, 30   2. 2, 5, 8, ____, 14, 17, 20, 23

3. 2, 4, 6, 20, _____, 60, 200, 400, 600, 2,000, 4,000

4. 100,000, 10,000, _____, 100, 10, 1

Find the next number in each sequence

1. 1, 3, 5, 7, _____   2. 3, 6, 9, 12, 15, _____

3. 2, 4, 6, 8, _____   4. 35, 40, 45, 50, _____

Alternate numbers with the letters of the alphabet from A to Z

1. Count by 2's

2. Count by 3's

3. Count by 5's

4. Count by 10's

True or False

1. Counting by 2s represents an increasing pattern.

2. A countdown is considered to be a repeating pattern.

Shapes/Patterns Quiz

1.

How many squares are repeated in the pattern?

How many triangles are repeated in the pattern?

2.

How many circles repeat in this pattern?

How many diamond shapes repeat?

Complete the following patterns:

1. 1, 3, 4, 7, 11, _____

2. 2, 4, 6, 12, 14, 16, 22, 24 _____

3. 81, 72, 63, 54, _____

Fill in the blanks:

1.

2.   5, 10, 15, _____, 25, _____, 35, 40

3.   3, 7, 10, 17, 27, _____

True or False

1.   If the following pattern continues, the next shape will be rectangle.

     Rectangle, square, triangle, rectangle, square, triangle, rectangle, _____

2.   Counting by fives produces two patterns: an increasing pattern and a repeating   odd and even pattern.

Length

The standard system of measuring length in the United States uses inches, feet, yards, and miles. Based on the length or distance being measured, a different unit is chosen.

For example, to describe how far one city is from another, it would be more appropriate to use miles rather than inches. However, inches would be more appropriate for measuring the length of a small table. Feet are often used to measure a person's height and yards are commonly used for measuring plots of land like football fields, which are 100 yards long.

Length Equivalents

Similar to other types of measurement, the different lengths have equivalent amounts to each other. The following list shows the various Standard Unit Lengths and how they relate to one another:

12 Inches = 1 Foot

3 Feet = 1 Yard   36 Inches = 1 Yard

1,760 Yards = 1 Mile   5,280 Feet = 1 Mile

Based on the above information, answer the following questions with the appropriate measurement:

1.   To figure out the length of ribbon needed to wrap a birthday present, do you use   yards or inches?

Inches are a better unit of measurement because the amount of ribbon needed is closer to inches than yards.

2.   To measure the size of a living room floor to see if a special rug will fit, is it   better to use miles or feet?

Feet are a more appropriate unit of measurement for a room. Miles are used to measure larger lengths and distances.

3.   To calculate the distance between Houston, Texas and New York City, New   York, is it better to use feet or miles?

Miles are a better unit of measurement because the length or distance from Houston to New York is much greater than the size of a foot.

4   To figure out the length of a strip of land to determine if a new football field can   be installed, are inches or yards a better unit of measurement?

Yards are a better unit of measurement because the length of a football field is generally measured in 10-yard sections up to a total of 100 yards.

In school, students practice measuring items using a ruler with 1-inch markings up to 12 inches. The inches are also divided in half and have marking associated with them so students can measure items smaller than 1 inch. Answer the following measurement questions based on the use of a standard 12-inch ruler:

1.   Jamie measures two pencils using his ruler. One measures 3 inches and the other   measures 2 and 1/2 inches. Which one is shorter in length?

The pencil that is 2 and 1/2 inches is shorter.

2.   Which is closer to a foot in length: 7 inches or 13 inches?

13 inches, although greater than one foot, is only 1 inch from 12 inches (1 foot) and 7 inches is 5 inches away from a foot. So, 13 inches is closer to 1 foot than 7 inches.

3.   One book measures 8 and 1/2 inches wide and another measures 9 inches across.   Which   book has a larger width?

The book that measures 9 inches across has a larger width than the book that measures 8 and 1/2 inches.

4.   How many 12-inch rulers would a student need to measure an item that was 18   inches   long?

One whole 12-inch ruler and 6 more inches of a second ruler would be needed to measure an item 18 inches long.

Standard Length Units and Metric Length Units

The student would need two rulers and would measure the entire 12 inches of one and then 6 inches of the second to be able to accurately measure the item.

Although in the United States we mainly use the Standard Units of Length to measure items and distances, the Metric System is used on occasion and is used frequently throughout the world. The Metric System uses millimeters, centimeters, meters, and kilometers to measure lengths and distances.

Below is a list of general equivalents between the Standard Units of Length and the Metric Units of Length:

1 meter is approximately 2 1/2 feet

1 mile is approximately 2 kilometers

1 inch is approximately 2 1/2 centimeters

Based on the their approximate equivalents, answer the following questions comparing Standard Units and Metric Units:

1.   Which is greater: 1 Meter or 1 Inch?   If 1 Meter is approximately 2 1/2 feet and it takes   12 inches to equal 1 foot, 1 Meter is greater than 1 Inch.

2.   If miles are used to measure the distance between cities, which is the similar Metric Unit: Centimeters or Kilometers? Since, 1 mile is approximately equal to 2 Kilometers and 2 1/2 Centimeters is approximately 1 Inch, the similar metric unit to Miles is Kilometers.

3.   If it is better to measure a room in feet, which Metric Unit would also be used to measure the length of a room? Since 2 1/2 feet equal 1 meter, the Metric Unit to measure the length of a room would be the Meter.

4.   If a town is 12 miles from the nearest grocery store, approximately how many kilometers from the grocery store is the town? Since, 1 mile is approximately 2 kilometers, the grocery store and town are about 24 kilometers apart.

5.   A student measures himself to be 5 feet tall. Approximately, how many meters tall is the student? Since there approximately 2 1/2 feet per meter, the student is about 2 meters tall.

In summary, whether using Standard Units or Metric Units, the following concepts need to be remembered by

Second Grade students:

- Inches and Centimeters are the best units to measure the length of smaller items like books, pencils, ribbon, shoe size, etc.
- Feet and Meters are best for measuring the length moderately sized objects and items like the length of a room, the size of a ping-pong table, the proper length for curtains, etc.
- Miles and Kilometers are best for measuring distances between neighbors, towns, and cities.
- Generally, heights are measured in feet and meters.

Length – Practice Sheet

1 meter is approximately 2 1/2 feet	12 Inches = 1 Foot	
1 mile is approximately 2 kilometers	3 Feet = 1 Yard	36 Inches = 1 Yard
1 inch is approximately 2 1/2 centimeters	1,760 Yards = 1 Mile	5,280 Feet = 1 Mile

Standard Length Units

1. Which is greater, 12 inches or 2 feet?

2. Which is greater, 3 feet or 3 yards?

3. Which is smaller, 12 inches or 1 foot?

4. A Person's height is usually measured in _____.

5. The height of a mountain is usually measured in _____.

6. Which is greater 12 yards or 1 mile?

7. Would a student measure his height using inches or miles?

8. Which is a better unit of measure for determining the distance between two cities,   inches   or miles?

9. How many feet are in 1 yard?

10. How many feet in 1 mile?

Metric Length Units

1. Which is longer, 1 meter or 1 centimeter?

2. which is better for measuring distances between cities, centimeters or kilometers?

3. Which is better for measuring the length of a spoon, centimeters or meters?

4. Which is better for measuring the length of a driveway, kilometers or meters?

Comparing Standard and Metric Length Units

1. Which is greater, inches or meters?

2   Which is smaller, feet or kilometers?

3.   Which Standard and Which Metric Units are best for measuring the distance   between San Diego and Los Angeles?

4. Approximately, how many centimeters are in 1 inch?

5. Approximately, how many kilometers in 1 mile?

6. Approximately how many feet in 1 meter?

Length – Quiz

1. Which Standard Unit is better for measuring the distance between two windows   of a house?

2. Which Standard Unit is best for measuring the length of fabric needed to re-cover   several pieces of furniture?

3. Which Standard Unit is best for determining how far San Francisco is from New   York City?

4. Which Standard Unit is generally used for measuring a person's height?

5. How many inches in 1 foot?

6. How many feet in 1 yard?

7. Which are similar in length, miles and centimeters or meters and feet?

8. Which are used for measuring long distances, miles and kilometers or inches and   centimeters?

9. Approximately, how many kilometers in 1 mile?

10. Approximately, how many centimeters are in 1 inch?

Weight/Capacity

Measuring the weight and capacity of objects and items is a daily occurrence in most households. For example, most mornings, people weigh themselves before dressing for work or school, people with special dietary needs weigh their food to be sure they are getting the proper amount of specific nutrients, the volume of water poured into a coffee maker has to match the capacity of the machine so it does not overflow, and the capacity of a tent needs to be known before heading out on a camping trip.

Weight is the measurement of how heavy something is and capacity is the measurement of the inside of an object to determine how much "stuff" it can hold. Both weight and capacity are measured in the United States by using Standard Units of Weight and Standard Units of Volume. The Standard Units for Weight are ounces, pounds, and tons. The Standard Units for Capacity are cups, pints, quarts and gallons.

Standard Units of Weight

The units of measurement for weight are based on the size and anticipated weight of an object or item. The material an object or item is made of also determines which unit of measure will be used to describe the weight.

For example, if a bag of feathers and the same size bag of concrete bricks are going to be weighed, which one is expected to be heavier? Well, based on the experience of feathers being much lighter than concrete bricks, it is anticipated that the bag full of bricks will be heavier.

The table below lists the Standard Units of Weight and common items those units measure:

OUNCES	Individual Fruit and Vegetables, flour and sugar for baking, baby animals, sliced cheese and deli meats, wool and yarn.
POUNDS	Bunches of fruits and vegetables, turkeys, potatoes, bundles of firewood, bags of grain, people, backpacks, books, coffee.
TONS	Cars and trucks, elephants, logs, piles of bricks,

Weight Comparisons and Equivalents

In Standard Units of Weight, the order of smallest to greatest unit of measure is ounces, pounds, and tons: ounces being the smallest unit of measure and tons being the largest. Since pounds fall somewhere in between ounces and tons, it is the most popular unit of measure.

Based on the above information, answer the following questions:

1. Which unit would be used to measure the weight of an apple? Since apples are relatively small and light, they would be weighed using ounces.

2. Which unit would be used to measure a truck carrying a load of bricks to a construction site? Since a truck carrying bricks is considered to be very heavy, it would be weighed using tons.

3. Is a golf ball more likely to weigh 2 ounces or 2 pounds? Since a golf ball is relatively light and needs to be aerodynamic, it is more likely to weigh 2 ounces.

4. Is a bicycle more likely to weigh 15 pounds or 15 tons? Since a bicycle is a moderately-sized item, it is more likely to weigh 15 pounds.

To convert between ounces and pounds, and between pounds and tons, refer to the following information:

16 ounces (oz) = 1 pound (lb)

2,000 lbs = 1 Ton (T)

Convert between Standard Units of Weight

1. How many ounces of ice cream are needed to make 2 lbs? Since it takes 16 oz to make 1 lb, it will require 32 oz to make 2 lbs of ice cream.

2. How many pounds does a 3-Ton boulder weigh? Since there are 2,000 lbs in 1T, there are 6,000lbs in 3T.

Metric Units of Weight (Mass)

Although Standard Units of Weight are the units of choice most of the time in the United States, sometimes Metric Units of Weight (Mass) are used. So, it is important to be introduced to Metric Units of Weight early in a student's education.

The following Metric Units and their similar Standard Units of Weight have been matched:

2 pounds are approximately 1 kilogram

1 ounce equals approximately 30 grams

Generally, pounds and kilograms are the most widely used units of weight measurement. Based on the above conversion information, indicate approximate equivalent weights for the items described below:

1.   How many pounds is a table that weighs 5 kilograms? Since each kilogram is equal to about 2 pounds, the approximate weight of the table is 10 pounds.

2.   How many ounces is 90 grams? Since there is 1 oz for each 30 grams, then 90   grams is approximately 3oz.

3.   Approximately how many kilograms does a 50-pound desk weigh? Since there is   one kilogram per 2 lbs, the desk weighs about 25 kilograms.

Standard Units for Capacity

Capacity is the amount of a substance in a container. These containers have the following Standard Capacities from smallest to largest: cups, pints, quarts, and gallons. These units are used to measure numerous amounts of substances daily in most households. For example, a typical breakfast may consist of a cup of milk with a bowl of cereal, to make chocolate chip cookies the ingredients are usually measured using cups, and when milk or juice is purchased at the store, they are usually packaged in gallon and 1/2 gallon containers.

Comparing Units of Capacity

For the following items, decide which unit of measurement is best:

1.   Is the capacity of a swimming pool better measured in gallons or pints? Since a   pool can hold a very large amount of water, gallons are the best unit of   measurement.

2.   When adding water to a small fish tank, would it be better to add a few cups or   several quarts? Since the fish tank is described as being small, using cups to add   water would be the best choice.

3.   A mom is making hot chocolate for her two children. Is it better for her to use cups to measure the amount of hot chocolate per child or gallons? Since the mom   is making hot chocolate to be consumed by just two children and not a large group of people, cups is the better unit of measure.

Sometimes, these units of measure need to be converted one to another and the following list indicates the proper conversions:

2 cups = 1 pint

2 pints = 1 quart

4 quarts = 1 gallon

Calculate the proper amounts in the following problems:

1.   If a recipe calls for 2 quarts of milk, how many pints will the recipe need? Since 2 pints equal 1 quart, then 4 pints equal 2 quarts and 4 pints would be needed for the   recipe.

2.   Water needs to be available to the competitors of a foot race. If there are 16 cups   in a gallon, how many gallons will be needed to produce at least 64 cups? If 16   cups make a gallon and 64 cups can be divided into 4 groups of 16 cups, then 4   gallons of water will be needed for the race.

3.   If 3 gallons of paint is used to cover the inside walls of 3 bedrooms, how many   quarts of paint does that amount equal? Since there are 4 quarts per gallon, then 3   gallons yields 12 quarts.

Metric Units for Capacity

The most popular unit of measurement in the Metric System is the Liter (l). The closest Standard Unit of Measurement is the gallon. One gallon equals approximately 2 liters.

Understanding the approximate equivalent of 2 liters to 1 gallon, solve the following conversion problems:

1.   Several people will be attending a party. If the hosts have a 5-gallon container   from which soda-pop will be dispensed, how many 2-liter bottles of soda-pop will   they need?   Since 1 gallon is approximately equal to 1 2-liter container, 5 2- liter bottles will need to be purchased.

2.   Each student going on a field trip needs to bring a 1-liter container of water to   drink. How many gallons will the teacher need to fill 20 liters? Since there are   approximately 2 liters per gallon, the teacher will need to use 10 gallons of water.

Summary

Whether students use Standard Units of Measurement for weight and capacity or Metric Units of Measurement for weight and capacity, understanding when to use which unit is the most important concept.

In other words, smaller units for smaller, lighter items and objects, and larger units for larger items and objects.

Standard Units for Weight smallest to biggest = ounces, pounds, tons

Metric Units for Weight smallest to biggest = grams, kilograms

Standard Units for Capacity smallest to biggest = cups, pints, quarts, gallons

Metric Unit used most often for Capacity = liter

Weight/Capacity – Practice Sheet

1.   A fully loaded logging truck stops to be weighed. Will its weight be measured in   tons or pounds?

2.   Several students weigh themselves for a science experiment. Should their weight be   recorded in pounds or ounces?

3.   A pizza parlor weighs the amount of shredded cheese it uses for each pizza. Do   they use ounces of cheese or pounds of cheese per pizza?

4.   What is the order of the Standard Units for Weight from lightest to heaviest?

16 ounces (oz) = 1 pound (lb)

2,000 lbs = 1 Ton (T)

5.   How many ounces are in 2 pounds?

6.   How many Tons will 6,000 pounds create?

7.   How many pounds will 48 ounces create?

2 pounds are approximately 1 kilogram

32 ounces are approximately 1 kilogram

1 ounce equals approximately 30 grams

8.   If a great big science book weighs 4 pounds, approximately how many kilograms   does it   weigh?

9.   2 kilograms equals approximately how many ounces?

10   A 2-ounce golf ball weighs approximately how many grams?

11. Which units of weight (standard and metric) would be best for measuring how   much a ball of yarn weighs?

2 cups = 1 pint

2 pints = 1 quart

4 quarts = 1 gallon

12. If 6 pints of cream are needed for a pie recipe, how many quarts should be used?

13. 20 gallons of punch are needed for a party. How many quarts can be used?

14. How many cups will 15 pints of apple juice produce?

15. How many pints equal one gallon?

16. Which is the best unit of measure to determine the capacity of a swimming pool?

17. Which unit of capacity is best for measuring how much sugar is needed for a cake recipe?

18. Is it more likely to find quarts of juice at the store or cups?

19. How many liters equal approximately 1 gallon?

20. Are gallons or liters of soda-pop sold in the average grocery store?

Weight/Capacity – Quiz

16 ounces (oz) = 1 pound (lb) 2,000 lbs = 1 Ton (T)	2 pounds are approximately 1 kilogram 32 ounces are approximately 1 kilogram 1 ounce equals approximately 30 grams 1 gallon is approximately 2 Liters	2 cups = 1 pint 2 pints = 1 quart 4 quarts = 1 gallon

1. Which of the above units represent the Standard Units for Weight?

2. How many Liters approximately equal 1 gallon?

3. In an Ice Cream eating contest the winner ate a total of 8 pints. How many quarts did the winner eat?

4. Twelve cups of pineapple are needed for a special recipe. How many 1-quart cans of pineapple are required?

5. Approximately, how many liters of water will be needed to fill 8 1-gallon containers?

6. A wheelbarrow carries a small pile of bricks to the backyard of a home to build a new fire pit. Should the bricks be weighed using pounds or ounces?

7. Approximately how many pounds does a 5-kilogram package weigh?

8. How many cups are needed for a recipe that calls for 6 pints of cream?

9. A huge slap of stone that weighs 3 tons is going to be carved into a statue. The artist has to pay for the stone by the pound. How many pounds does he have to pay for?

10. If an item weighs 2 kilograms, approximately how many ounces does it weigh?

Probability

Probability is the study of "what if?" In other words, if a specific scenario is presented, what is likely or unlikely to occur when certain elements are introduced. Or, what is the likelihood of something happening based on a specific set of circumstances.

For example, is it more likely or less likely that you will see a giraffe walking down the middle of the street in New York City? Since giraffes are not native to New York City, the fact that New York City is not located in Africa, and if, the zoo in New York City did house giraffes, it would be almost impossible for them to escape, it is less likely that you will see a giraffe walking down the middle of the street in New York City.

Likely, Unlikely, Equally Likely

In Second Grade students are presented with the concept of probability by assessing whether an occurrence of an event is likely to happen or unlikely to happen, and if there is a choice between two outcomes of a test, whether one outcome is more likely, less likely, or if both outcomes are equally likely. First, the concept of the probability of an event occurring during specific circumstances is learned.

The following examples express the concepts of likely or unlikely:

1. The sun is shining and the sky is a beautiful clear blue. Is it likely or unlikely to   rain?

    It is unlikely to rain because the description of the day indicates no clouds and a   lot of bright sunshine.

2. It is a very hot day and the power has gone out in a neighborhood that has a large   neighborhood pool. Is it likely or unlikely that all the neighbors will go   swimming?

    It is very likely the pool will be crowded because the pool would be a great place   to stay   cool if the weather is very hot.

3. The students of a second grade math class have studied very hard for an upcoming test. All of them pass and get above 80% on their pre-tests. It is likely or unlikely   the majority students will pass the test with at least 80% correct?

    It is likely that the majority of the students will pass with at least 80% because of   the positive results of the pre-test.

4.   A certain baseball player hits a homerun 2 times for each 10 times at bat. It is likely or unlikely that on any given pitch, this baseball player will get a homerun?

       It is unlikely because he only gets a homerun a couple times for every 10 times he is at-bat.

In addition to determining if a single event is likely or unlikely, students will need to assess the probability of which one of two possible outcomes is more likely, less likely, or if both outcomes are equally likely. The following examples illustrate this concept of less likely, more likely, or equally likely:

1.   Two basketball teams are playing the final game of the season. Whichever team   wins will get the first place trophy. If team A has 4 players over 6 feet tall and   team B has 1 player over 6 feet tall, which team is more likely to win? If the   players are all equally skilled, it is more likely team A will win because more of their players can reach the basket and block the ball more easily due to their   height advantage.

2.   A dartboard is covered in the color blue with the exception of a very small spot of red in t   he middle. On which color is a dart more likely to land? A dart is more   likely to land on the blue color because it covers a much greater area of the   dartboard.

3.   If a bag contains 4 blue marbles and 4 red marbles, how likely is it that a blue marble will be blindly chosen? Since the number of blue marbles and the number   of red marbles is the same, there is an equal chance that either color will be chosen.

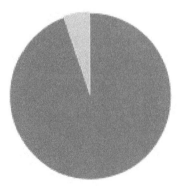

4.   If paintballs were shot at the above target, would they be more likely to hit the   light gray area or the dark

gray area? Since the dark gray area is greater in size   and easier to hit, it is more likely that the paintballs will hit the dark gray area   than the light gray area.

Certain, Probable, Unlikely, Impossible

Based on certain information, students will be able to determine whether an event is certain, probable, unlikely, or impossible. For example, if a bed of flowers is filled completely with only red flowers, the likelihood of finding a white flower is Impossible. Conversely, the likelihood of finding a red flower in the flowerbed is certain.

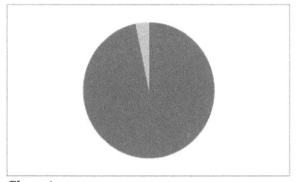

Chart A

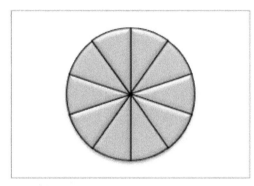

Chart B

Based Chart A, is it probable or unlikely that an arrow would strike the light gray area? Since the light gray area is significantly smaller than the dark gray area it makes it a much more difficult area to hit. Therefore, it is unlikely that an arrow will strike the light gray area. Because the light gray area exists within the dark gray area, the possibility exists that it could be struck so it cannot be considered impossible. Similarly, it cannot be considered certain that the dark gray area will be struck.

Although similar to Chart A, Chart B represents a set of probabilities that are both impossible and certain. An arrow shot at this target will certainly hit the gray area. The likelihood that an arrow will strike a different color is therefore, impossible.

Other situations that involve impossible and certain probabilities occur every day. Examples include the following:

1. It is certain that the sun will not be seen at night.

2. It is impossible for a dog to have a litter of kittens.

3. It is certain that a fire in the fireplace is extremely hot.

4. It is impossible for ice to catch fire.

5. It is certain that the earth has only one moon.

6. It is impossible for humans to breathe naturally underwater.

Students will use math and probability equations to determine the probable occurrence of specific events with better accuracy later in elementary school and middle school.

Probability – Practice Sheet

True or False

1. If an event is considered to be likely to occur, then it will definitely occur every   time the test is conducted.

2. If an event is considered to be unlikely, then although it will not occur often, the   possibility that the event could occur does exist.

3. When an event is certain to occur, there is still a small chance it will not occur on   occasion.

4. When an event is considered to be impossible, it will never occur as long as the   circumstances remain the same.

More Likely, Less Likely, Equally Likely

1. A spinner used for playing board games is half red and half blue. What is the   likelihood that the arrow will land in the blue area?

2. During the winter months in Michigan, what is the likelihood that it will snow?

3. During the hot summer months in the desert, what is the likelihood of rain?

4. A bag full of jellybeans has 100 red jellybeans and 5 yellow jellybeans. Which   color is more likely to be grabbed in a handful?

5. A deck of cards has exactly 4 kings and 4 queens. If only these 8 cards are used,   what is the likelihood of drawing a king rather than a queen?

6. A teacher hands out pencils to her class to take a test. There are forty students and 50 pencils. If only two of the pencils are sharpened, what is the likelihood that a   student will get a sharpened pencil?

7. A tennis champion has won 9 out of the last 10 matches against his opponent. Is it more likely or less likely that he will win the next match against this same   opponent?

8. If a second grade student reaches into a bag containing the last 10 chocolate bars   and last 3 lollipops from Halloween, which sweet treat is more likely to be   grabbed?

9.   Mr. Smith has carved the Smith Family Thanksgiving turkey for the last 8   Thanksgiving dinners. It is more likely or less likely that he will carve the turkey   again this year?

10. Madison watches cartoon everyday after school for a half-hour before doing her   homework. Is it more or less likely she will do her homework before watching   cartoons tomorrow after school?

Certain, Probable, Unlikely, Impossible

1.   The sun rises in the east and sets in the west. What is the likelihood that it will   rise in the west tomorrow morning?

2.   A robin lays three eggs in the spring. What is the likelihood that all three chicks   will be baby robins?

3.   A monarch caterpillar spins a cocoon and undergoes the change into a butterfly.   What is the likelihood that it will emerge as a Blue Morpho butterfly?

4.   A bag contains 25 black checkers and 1 red checker. What is the likelihood that a   black checker will be blindly chosen?

5.   A dozen chocolate chip cookies are made with semi-sweet chocolate chips. What   is the likelihood that there will be a cookie with white chocolate chips?

6.   A package of cherry popsicles is purchased at the store. What is the likelihood   that when opened the package will contain grape popsicles?

Probability – Quiz

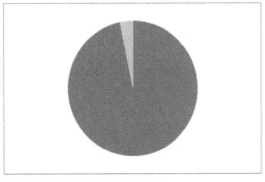

Chart 1   Chart 2

1. Which graph shows the possibility of two event outcomes?

2. Which graph shows either a certain outcome or an impossible outcome?

3. In Chart 1, which color depicts the less likely outcome?

4. What is the likelihood of an arrow hitting a white slice on Graph 2?

5. What is the likelihood of a paintball striking the dark gray area on Chart 1?

6. If the light gray portion of Chart 1 was increased to cover half of the circle, would the likelihood of it being struck by a paintball increase or decrease?

7. A box of crayons contains 20 purple and 20 orange colored crayons. If a student   reaches into the box without looking into it, what is the likelihood that an orange   crayon will be chosen opposed to a purple crayon?

8. A teacher passes out a spelling test. All the students passed the pre-test given the   day before. Is it more or less likely that all of the students will pass the test.?

9. A newspaper boy always throws the paper so it lands on the front porch of a   specific house. When he delivers his paper tomorrow morning, what is the   likelihood that the paper he throws lands on the front porch again?

10. As the earth circles the sun, seasons change in certain parts of the world. The cycle is winter, spring, summer, and fall. What is the possibility that summer will follow winter next year?

Graphs

Data is constantly being collected and interpreted throughout our modern society. Each night, if we watch the news programs, the weather report is usually presented. The meteorologists measure and interpret numerous groups of data to assess what the upcoming days will be like with regard to temperature, wind speed, cloud cover, rain, etc. The weather map we see on the news is essentially a weather graph.

Students in second grade will begin to learn how to read a variety of types of graphs and interpret the data presented. The types of graphs students will learn and use include coordinate graphs, bar graphs, pictographs, line plots, and line graphs.

Coordinate Graphs

The graph presented below is known as a Coordinate Graph. A vertical number and a horizontal number are paired into what are called coordinates. These coordinates are then plotted on a graph as a single location.

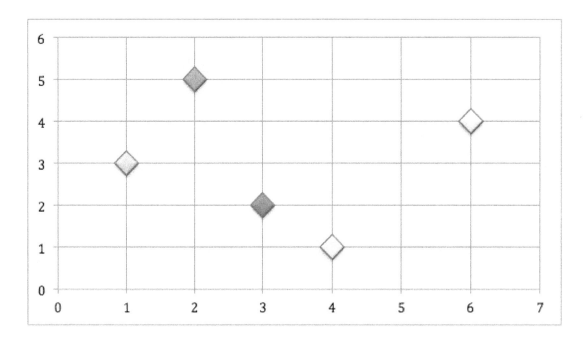

The Coordinate Graph above has 5 points plotted in a variety of locations. The following coordinates and their respective colored points are represented:

Descriptive Coordinate Location	Proper Coordinate Location
Violet is located at 1 across and 3 up.	Violet is at (1,3)
Red is located at 2 across and 5 up.	Red is at (2,5)
Blue is located at 3 across and 2 up.	Blue is at (3,2)
Green is located at 4 across and 1 up.	Green is at (4,1)
Yellow is located at 6 across and 4 up.	Yellow is at (6,4)

The first number in the proper coordinate is the horizontal number and the second number is for the vertical number.

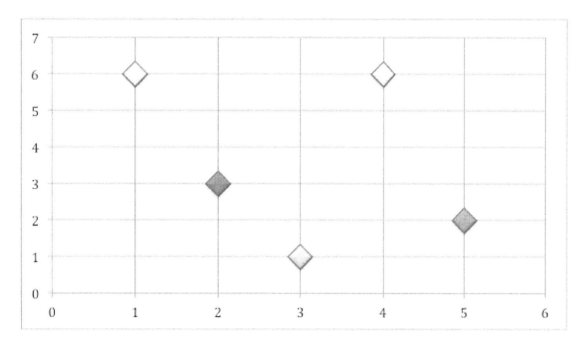

For the above graph, pair up the color of the coordinate with its horizontal and vertical numbers:

Green   (1,6)Blue(2,3)Violet   (3,1)Yellow   (4,6)   Red (5,2)

By looking at the locations of each of these colored points, the student can make some interpretations:

1.   The yellow and green points are the closest to the top of the graph.

2.   The violet point is located closest to the bottom of the graph.

3.   The red point is the farthest to the right on the graph.

4.   The green point and the red point are farthest apart.

5.   The blue point and the violet point are closest together.

6.   The horizontal coordinate for the green, violet and red points are odd.

7. The yellow point is the only coordinate with two even numbers.

Bar Graphs

Another type of graph students will use is the Bar Graph. This type of graph is very easy to read because it displays collected data very clearly. The taller the bar, the bigger the number or the greater the quantity of data.

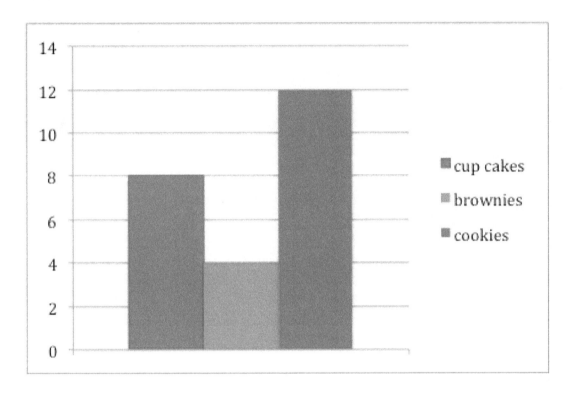

The above graph was created from the following data:

Item	Number Sold
Cupcakes	8
Brownies	4
Cookies	12

Information that can be gathered from this table and graph combination includes the following:

1. The greatest number of goods sold are the cookies.

2. The fewest goods sold are the brownies.

3. Four more cupcakes were sold than brownies and four more cookies were sold   than cupcakes.

4.   Cookies were the most popular item and brownies were the least popular item.

Based o the above information, some conclusions can be approximated:

1.   More people like cookies than brownies and cupcakes.

2.   The cookies may have been less expensive than the cupcakes and brownies.

3.   The cupcakes and brownies may have been larger and were shared by a couple   people and the cookies were smaller and enjoyed by individuals.

Pictographs

Pictographs are another form of presenting data in an easily understandable visual format. Items are used in a table format to represent certain quantities of that item.

Betty	🥚 🥚 🥚
Lucy	🥚
Sally	🥚 🥚 🥚 🥚 🥚
Amy	🥚 🥚
Kathy	🥚 🥚 🥚

The above pictograph represents 5 hens and the number of eggs they laid over 5 days.

Based on this graph, the following information can be collected:

1. Sally laid one egg each day.

2. Lucy only laid one egg over 5 days.

3. Amy laid one more egg than Lucy.

4. Betty and Kathy laid equal numbers of eggs.

5. Sally is the best producer of eggs in this hen house.

6. The total number of eggs produced in this hen house is 14.

Line Plots

Another graphing method that could be used for the above data with a couple of details added is called a Line Plot. The following Line Plot shows how many eggs per day were laid by the hens.

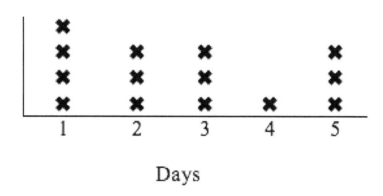

Days

This graph shows that only Lucy laid any eggs on Day 4, but that at least two other hens laid an egg on each of the other five days.

Line Graphs

The last type of graph to be covered is called a Line Graph. This graph shows several data points connected to form a continuous line.

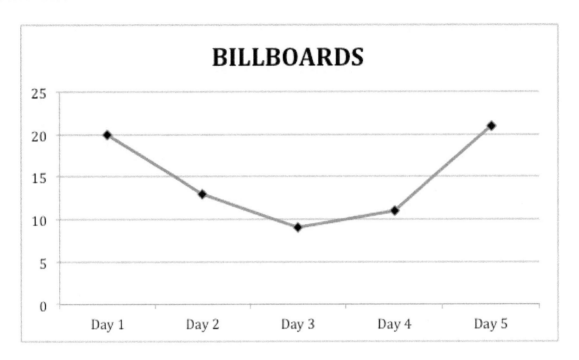

The above graph represents how many billboards a family counted per day on a five-day road trip. The following data can be gathered from the graph:

Day	Number of Billboards
1	20
2	between 10 and 15
3	just less than 10
4	just greater than 10
5	just greater than 20

Based on this data and the shape of the Line Graph, a few conclusions can be drawn:

1. The number of billboards counted on Day 1 and Day 5 are about double the number counted on the other three days.

2. The number of billboards counted dropped between Day 1 and Day 5.

3. Between Day 1 and Day 2, the number of billboards counted decreased.

4. Between Day 4 and Day 5, the number of billboards counted increased.

What could be one of the reasons for the decrease in the number of billboards counted between Day 1 and Day 2, a consistent lower number of billboards during Days 2, 3, and 4, and then an increase in the number of billboards between Days 4 and 5?

It is possible that the family traveled through a more rural area on Days 2, 3, and 4, and re-entered a more urban environment on Day 5.

Graphs – Practice Sheet

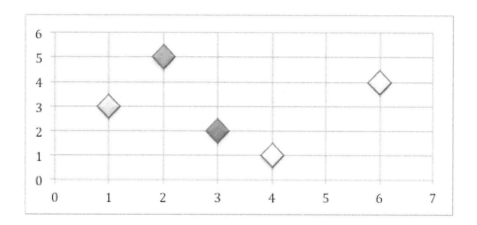

1. What type of graph is present above?

2. How many coordinates have been plotted?

3. Which color point has the greatest vertical value?

4. Which color point has 2 even coordinates?

5. Which color point is farthest left?

6. Which color point has the greatest horizontal coordinate?

Students
Eye Color

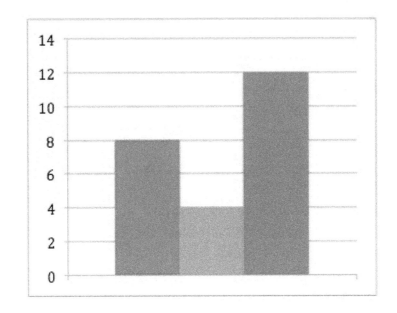

Based on the above graph, answer the following questions:

1. What type of graph is the graph above?

2. Which eye color do most students have?

3. How many more students have green eyes than brown?

4. How many more students have blue eyes than brown?

Types of Fruit Eaten at Breakfast for 7 days

Sarah	
Carlos	
Mason	
Karie	

1. What type of graph is presented above?

2. Which fruit did Sarah eat more of than the other students?

3. Which student ate the fewest bananas?

4. Which two fruits were consumed in equal total amounts?

Students choice of Favorite fruit

1. What type of graph is shown above?

2. Which fruit is most popular?

3. Which fruit is least popular?

4. If each ✖ equals two students, how many students were polled?

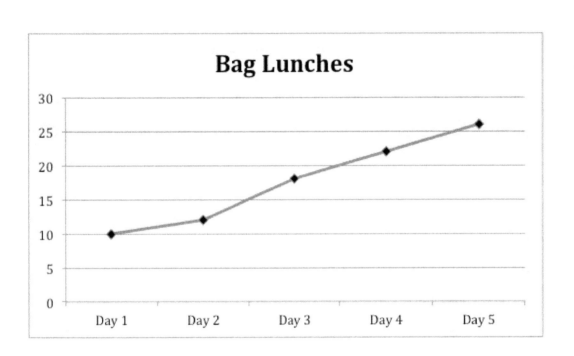

Bag Lunches

1. What type of graph is presented above?

2. Does the graph show an increase in bag lunches over 5 days or a decrease?

Graphs - Quiz

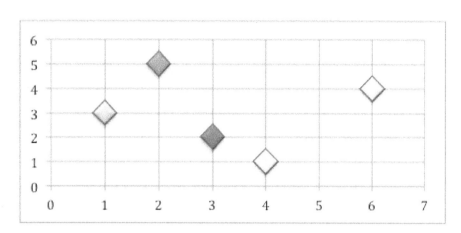

Graph A

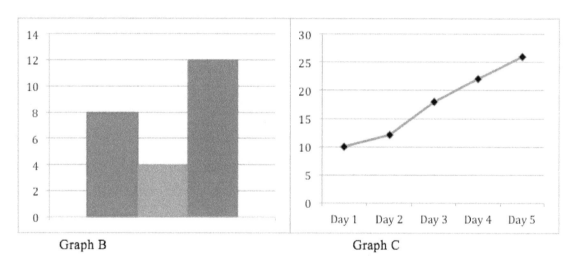

Graph B   Graph C

1. Which graph is a coordinate graph?

2. Which graph is a bar graph?

3. Which graph is a line graph?

4. Which graph shows a steady increase in data over time?

5. Which graph could show the square miles of water, flat land, and trees in an area   to be developed?

6. How many points are plotted on the coordinate graph?

7. How many data groups are used on the bar graph?

8. Which two graphs could be converted one into the other easily?

9. Which two graphs previously discussed are missing?

10. True or False, graphs allow the student to visually asses a variety of data?

Answer Key

Number Sense – Practice Sheet

1. What is the place value for the number three in 3,526?   thousands

2. What is the place value for the number 7 in 743?   hundreds

3. What is the place value for the zero in 107?   Tens

4. Circle the whole numbers: 3, 4.3, 6, ½, 7.1, 9/10   Answer: 3 and 6

5. True or False: 4 3/4 is a whole number.   False

Number Names

1. Write the name for 205.   Two hundred five

2. Write the name for 1,706.   One thousand, seven hundred six

3. Write the number for Three thousand, fifty-two. 3, 052

4. Write the name for 47th Forty-seventh

5. Write the number for Eighty-Eighth   88th

6. Round 47 to the closest Tens Place: 50

Odds and Evens

1. Is 237 odd or even?   odd

2. Is 425 odd or even?   odd

3. Is 562 odd or even?   even

4.   If you count by three's are all the numbers odd? No. every other number is   even.

5.   If you count by four's are all the numbers even? yes

Comparing Numbers

1.   Is 51 greater than or less than 15? Greater than

2.   Which is the 3rd number after 10? 13

3.   Which five numbers are between 12 and 18?   13, 14, 15, 16, and 17

4.   How many zeros are in One Thousand?   3

5.   How many tens (count by tens) are between Twenty and Fifty? 2 (30 and 40)

Number Sense - Quiz

1.   Write the name for 2,358   Two thousand, three hundred fifty-eight

2.   Write the name for 637 Six hundred thirty-seven

3.   Round 84 to the nearest Tens Place: 80

4.   Write the number for Seventy-Ninth   79th

5.   Which numbers are in between 23 and 27? 24, 25, and 26

6.   Which number is even: 14 or 17 14

7.   Which number is greater: 23 or 32 32

8.   Fill in the missing number: 2   4   _____   8   10   Answer: 6

9.   If you come in 7th place in a race, how many people came in to the finish before   you? Answer: 6

10. Which number is less than 27:   26 or 28 Answer: 26

Addition and Subtraction - Practice Sheet

Fill in the missing numbers:

1. 1 + 3 = 4   2. 2 + 5 = 7

    3 + ___ = 4   [1]   ___ + 2 = 7   [5]

    4 – 1 = 3   7 - ___ = 2   [5]

    4 - ___ = 1   [3]   7 - ___ = 5   [2]

Solve (remember to line up proper places or columns to get the correct answer)

1. 12 + 1 = [13] 2. 32 + 84 =   [116]   3. 810 + 21 =   [831]

4. 90 – 12 =   [78] 5. 98 – 15 =[83] 6. 992 – 827 = [165]

7. 85 + 95 =   [180]   8. 410 + 127 = [537]   9. 321 + 620 = [941]

10. 87 – 18 =[69] 11. 726 – 552 = [74] 12. 565 – 221 = [344]

13. 97 + 12 =[109]   14. 123 + 456 = [579]   15. 722 + 32 =   [754]

Greater Than, Less Than, Equal To

1. 12 + 14 + 1 _____30 – 3   =

2. 125 − 18 _____ 100 + 2 + 3   >

3. 715 − 113 _____ 300 + 200 + 157   <

Addition and Subtraction - Quiz

Fill In the Blanks

1.   12 + _____ = 17, _____ + 12 = 17, 17 - _____ = 12, 17 – 12 = _____   [5]

2.   23 + _____ = 50, _____ + 23 = 50, 50 - _____ = 23, 50 – 23 = _____   [27]

Solve

1.   871 + 123 =   [994]

2.   726 – 13 =   [713]

3.   35 + 27 =[62]

4.   872 – 773 =   [99]

5.   73 + 271 =   [344]

6.   956 – 897 =   [59]

7.   25 + 29 =[54]

8.   621 – 599 =   [22]

Fractions – Practice Sheet

1. How many pieces total are there in the above pie chart?   [8]

2. If you put the white piece and the darkest piece together what would be the   fraction? [2/8]

3. How many pieces equal 1/2 of the pie? [4]

4. What is the fraction for just one piece? [1/8]

5. If you picture the pie chart as a clock face, how many pieces equal 1/4 hour (15   min)? [2]

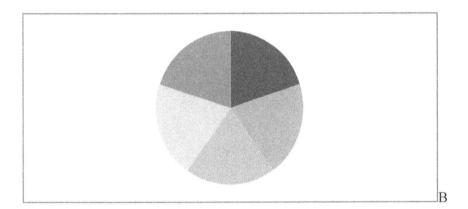

B

6. Is one piece from Chart A bigger or smaller than one piece from Chart B?   [smaller]

7. Which is bigger, 1/8 or 1/5? [1/5]

Answer the following questions using Chart A and Chart B:

8. Which is bigger, 3/5 or 4/8? [3/5]

9. If each chart were a real pie, which one would feed more guests? [A]

10. What is the denominator for Chart A? [8]   Chart B? [5]

Answer the following questions using the above set of shapes:

1. What is the total number of shapes?   [10]

2 How many squares are there?   [5]

3. Write the number of squares and the total number of shapes as a fraction: [5/10]

4. How many shapes are not circles? [8]

5. What fraction of the total shapes are circles?   [2/10]

6. What fraction of the total shapes are triangles?   [3/10]

Compare Fractions

7. Put these fractions in order of smallest to largest:2/3   2/7   2/5   [2/7,2/5,2/3]

8. Indicate whether the fractions are Greater Than, Less Than, or Equal: 7/7 ___ 3/3   [=]

9. Which Numerator is Greater: 5/16 or 9/10   [9/10]

10. Which Denominator is Greater: 1/8 or 4/7 [1/8]

Fractions - Quiz

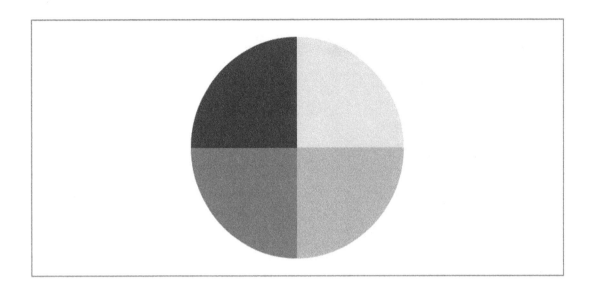

1. How many pieces are there in the above pie chart?   [4]

2. What fraction is the lightest color?   [1/4]

3. How many pieces make 1/2 of the pie chart?   [2]

4. What is the fraction for 3 of the four pieces? [3/4]

5. What denominator should be used for the above set of lightening bolts?   [6]

6. What is the fraction for the white lightening bolt?   [1/6]

7. What fraction of the lightening bolts are gray?   [3/6]

8. What fraction of the lightening bolts are black? [2/6]

Compare

9. Which is greater: 7/8 or 1/9[7/8]

10. How many of the fraction 1/16 are needed to make a fraction equal to 1? [16]

Operations – Practice Sheet

Place Values

1. What is the place value of the 8 in 185?   Tens

2. What is the place value of the 9 in 19? Ones

3. What is the place value of the 2 in 207?   Hundreds

4. What is the place value of the 4 in 4,123?   Thousands

Expanded Numbers

1. Write out the expanded number for 352: $300 + 50 + 2$

2. Write out the expanded number for 85: $80 + 5$

3. Write out the expanded number for 1,278: $1,000 + 200 + 70 + 8$

4. Write the standard number for $20 + 9$:   29

5. Write the standard number for $300 + 70 + 3$:   373

6. Write the standard number for $5,000 + 200 + 20 + 1$: 5,221

The clock above shows the hour hand on the 2 and the minute hand on the 12. The time represented is 2:00.

1. If it is during the day, is the time 2:00 AM or 2:00 PM?   2:00PM

2. If the minute hand is moved to the 6, is the time 2:15 or 2:30? 2:30

3. If the hour hand is moved to the 6, and it is after midnight but before noon, what   time is   it?   6:00 AM

4. If the time is 8:15 PM, is it also 1/4 after 8:00 PM or 1/4 to 8:00 PM?

    1/4 after

Calendar

1. Which day of the week begins with the letter W? Wednesday

2. How many days are in the weekend?   Two

3. Which days are the weekend days?   Saturday and Sunday

4. Which day is next after Thursday?   Friday

Multiplication and Division

1. If there are 3 groups of 5 apples to be shared, how many people get an apple? 15

2. If there are 25 pencils and 5 students, how many pencils will each student get?5

Operations – Quiz

1. What is the place value of the Zero in 1,027?   Hundreds

2. What is the place value of the 7 in 7,002?   Thousands

3. Write the standard number for 300 + 2 + 5:   325

4. Expand the number 7,329:   7000 + 300 + 20 + 9

5. Write an equivalent equation for 3 tens + 26 ones: 5 tens + 6 ones

6: If the time is 4:15 PM, what number is the hour hand pointing to?   4

7. If it is Tuesday, what is the name of the day to come next?   Wednesday

8. How many days per week do students go to school?   5

9. Since January is the first month of the year, what month is 4th?   April

10. Fill in the spaces: 5 x _____ = 50 AND 50 ÷ 5 = _____   10 for both

Money – Practice Sheet

Names and Amounts of Coins

1. Which coin has an amount of 25 cents?   Quarter

2. Which coin has the amount of 1 cent? Penny

3. What is the value of a dime?   Ten cents

4. What is the value of a nickel?   Five cents

5. How many quarters in One Dollar?   Four

6. How many dimes in One Dollar?   Ten

7. How many pennies in One Dollar?   One Hundred

8. How many nickels in one dime?   Two

9. How many pennies in one dime?   Ten

10. How many dimes in one quarter?   Two

Combinations and Amounts

1. How much money is 2 quarters and 3 pennies? $0.53 or 53¢

2. How much is 3 dimes, 2 nickels and 4 pennies? $0.44 or 44¢

3. How much is 3 quarters and 3 dimes? $1.05

4. How much is 2 Dollars and 4 dimes? $1.40

5. Which coins would be left if you started with 3 quarters and 3 dimes and spent 2   quarters and 1 dime?   1 quarter and 2 dimes

6. If you started with 6 dimes and 3 nickels and spent 2 dimes and 1 nickel, how many quarters could you exchange the remaining dimes and nickels for?   50 cents would be left so 2 quarters.

7. If Tim started with $3.89 and bought a book for $1.23, what would he have left? $2.66

8. If Joy started with $3.25 and earned $2.00 for walking the dog and $1.00 for   setting the table, how much will she have to go shopping? $6.25

9. How much money will Sam have at the end of the week if he earns $8.75 and spends $6.25? $2.50

10. If Josie starts with $9.85 and spends $7.38 on school supplies, how much would   she have left? $2.47

Money – Quiz

1. How many dimes equal the same amount as 6 quarters?   15

2. What is the name of the coin that is equal to 5 pennies?   Nickel

3. How many pennies in One Dollar?   100

4. How many nickels in 3 quarters? 15

5. What combination of quarters, dimes, and pennies is $0.98?

    3 quarters, 2 dimes, and 3 pennies

6. Write out the currency value for 3 quarters, 4 dimes, and 2 nickels: $1.25

7. If Danny earns $3.00 from his aunt, $2.50 from his Grandpa, and $1.25 from his   cousin, what would be the total amount of money Danny earned? $6.75

8. If Lisa has 6 quarters and 21 pennies, does she have enough money to buy a slice   of pizza for $1.75? No, 6 quarters = $1.50 and 21 pennies = $0.21 and only   equals $1.71

9. If Lisa borrows $0.20 from her friend Luke, what will her change be after buying   the pizza? $0.16

10. How much money will Brian have if he finds 2 quarters, 6 dimes, 4 nickels and 13 pennies? $1.43

Shapes/Patterns - Practice Sheet

Define the following types of Patterns [Answer: repeating, decreasing, and increasing]

Based on the above patterns, Answer the following questions:

1. What is the next shape in the first pattern?   square

2. What is the next shape in the second pattern?   circle

3. What is the next shape in the third pattern? star

Fill in the Blanks

1.   5, 10, _____, 20, 25, 30 [15]   2.   2, 5, 8, ____, 14, 17, 20, 23 [11]

3.   2, 4, 6, 20, _____, 60, 200, 400, 600, 2,000, 4,000 [40]

4.   100,000, 10,000, _____, 100, 10, 1   [1,000]

Find the next number in each sequence

1.   1, 3, 5, 7, _____   [9] 2.   3, 6, 9, 12, 15, _____ [18]

3.   2, 4, 6, 8, _____ [10] 4.   35, 40, 45, 50, _____ [55]

Alternate numbers with the letters of the alphabet from A to Z

1.   Count by 2's 2 A 4 B 6 C 8 D 10 E 12 F 14 G 16 H 18 I 20 J 22 K 24 L 26

2.   Count by 3's 3 A 6 B 9 C 12 D 15 E 18 F 21 G 24 H 27 I 30 J 33 K 36 L 39

3.   Count by 5's 5 A 10 B 15 C 20 D 25 E 30 F 35 G 40 H 45 I 50 J 55 K 60 L 65

4.   Count by 10's 10 A 20 B 30 C 40 D 50 E 60 F 70 G 80 H 90 I 100 J

True or False

1. Counting by 2s represents an increasing pattern. TRUE

2. A countdown is considered to be a repeating pattern. FALSE

Shapes/Patterns Quiz

How many squares are repeated in the pattern?   2

How many triangles are repeated in the pattern? 1

How many circles repeat in this pattern?   3

How many diamond shapes repeat?   1

Complete the following patterns:

1.   1, 3, 4, 7, 11, _____   [17]

2.   2, 4, 6, 12, 14, 16, 22, 24 _____   [26]

3.   81, 72, 63, 54, _____   [45]

Fill in the blanks:

2.   5, 10, 15, _____, 25, _____, 35, 40 [20, 30]

3.   3, 7, 10, 17, 27, _____   [44]

True or False

1.   If the following pattern continues, the next shape will be rectangle. FALSE

Rectangle, square, triangle, rectangle, square, triangle, rectangle, _____

2. Counting by fives produces two patterns: an increasing pattern and a repeating odd and even pattern.
    TRUE

Length – Practice Sheet

Standard Length Units

1. Which is greater, 12 inches or 2 feet?   [2 feet]

2. Which is greater, 3 feet or 3 yards?   [3 yards]

3. Which is smaller, 12 inches or 1 foot? (they are equal]

4. A Person's height is usually measured in _____.   [feet]

5. The height of a mountain is usually measured in _____.   [miles]

6. Which is greater 12 yards or 1 mile?   [1 mile]

7. Would a student measure his height using inches or miles? [inches]

8. Which is a better unit of measure for determining the distance between two cities,   inches   or miles? [miles]

9. How many feet are in 1 yard?   [3]

10. How many feet in 1 mile?   [5,280]

Metric Length Units

1. Which is longer, 1 meter or 1 centimeter?   [1 meter]

2. which is better for measuring distances between cities, centimeters or kilometers? [kilometers]

3. Which is better for measuring the length of a spoon, centimeters or meters?   [centimeters]

4. Which is better for measuring the length of a driveway, kilometers or meters? [meters]

Comparing Standard and Metric Length Units

1. Which is greater, inches or meters?   [meters]

2   Which is smaller, feet or kilometers?   [feet]

3.   Which Standard and Which Metric Units are best for measuring the distance   between San Diego and Los Angeles? [miles and kilometers]

4.   Approximately, how many centimeters are in 1 inch? [2 1/2]

5.   Approximately, how many kilometers in 1 mile? [2 1/2]

6.   Approximately how many feet in 1 meter?   [2 1/2]

Length – Quiz

1. Which Standard Unit is better for measuring the distance between two windows   of a house?   [inches]

2. Which Standard Unit is best for measuring the length of fabric needed to re-cover several pieces of furniture?   [yards]

3. Which Standard Unit is best for determining how far San Francisco is from New   York City?   [miles]

4. Which Standard Unit is generally used for measuring a person's height? [feet]

5. How many inches in 1 foot?

6. How many feet in 1 yard?

7. Which are similar in length, miles and centimeters or meters and feet?

   [meters and feet]

8. Which are used for measuring long distances, miles and kilometers or inches and   centimeters?   [miles and kilometers]

9. Approximately, how many kilometers in 1 mile? [2 1/2]

10. Approximately, how many centimeters are in 1 inch? [2 1/2]

Weight/Capacity – Practice Sheet

1. A fully loaded logging truck stops to be weighed. Will its weight be measured in   tons or pounds?   [tons]

2. Several students weigh themselves for a science experiment. Should their weight be   recorded in pounds or ounces?   [pounds]

3. A pizza parlor weighs the amount of shredded cheese it uses for each pizza. Do   they use ounces of cheese or pounds of cheese per pizza?   [ounces]

4. What is the order of the Standard Units for Weight from lightest to heaviest?

     [ounces, pounds, tons]

16 ounces (oz) = 1 pound (lb)

2,000 lbs = 1 Ton (T)

5. How many ounces are in 2 pounds?   [32]

6. How many Tons will 6,000 pounds create? [3]

7. How many pounds will 48 ounces create?   [3]

2 pounds are approximately 1 kilogram

32 ounces are approximately 1 kilogram

1 ounce equals approximately 30 grams

8. If a great big science book weighs 4 pounds, approximately how many kilograms   does it   weigh? [2]

9. 2 kilograms equals approximately how many ounces? [64]

10 A 2-ounce golf ball weighs approximately how many grams?   [60]

11. Which units of weight (standard and metric) would be best for measuring how   much a ball of yarn weighs? [ounces and grams]

2 cups = 1 pint

2 pints = 1 quart

4 quarts = 1 gallon

12. If 6 pints of cream are needed for a pie recipe, how many quarts should be used?   [3]

13. 20 gallons of punch are needed for a party. How many quarts can be used? [80]

14. How many cups will 15 pints of apple juice produce? [30]

15. How many pints equal one gallon?   [8]

16. Which is the best unit of measure to determine the capacity of a swimming pool?   [gallons]

17. Which unit of capacity is best for measuring how much sugar is needed for a cake recipe?   [cups]

18. Is it more likely to find quarts of juice at the store or cups? [quarts]

19. How many liters equal approximately 1 gallon? [2]

20. Are gallons or liters of soda-pop sold in the average grocery store?   [liters]

Weight/Capacity – Quiz

1. Which of the above units represent the Standard Units for Weight?   [ounces, pounds, tons]

2. How many Liters approximately equal 1 gallon? [2]

3. In an Ice Cream eating contest the winner ate a total of 8 pints. How many quarts   did the   winner eat?
   [4]

4. Twelve cups of pineapple are needed for a special recipe. How many 1-quart cans of pineapple are required?
   [3]

5. Approximately, how many liters of water will be needed to fill 8 1-gallon   containers?   [16]

6. A wheelbarrow carries a small pile of bricks to the backyard of a home to build a   new fire pit. Should the bricks be weighed using pounds or ounces?   [pounds]

7. Approximately how many pounds does a 5-kilogram package weigh?   [10]

8. How many cups are needed for a recipe that calls for 6 pints of cream?   [12]

9. A huge slap of stone that weighs 3 tons is going to be carved into a statue. The   artist has to pay for the stone by the pound. How many pounds does he have to   pay for?   [6,000 pounds]

10. If an item weighs 2 kilograms, approximately how many ounces does it weigh?   [64]

Probability – Practice Sheet

True or False

1. If an event is considered to be likely to occur, then it will definitely occur every   time the test is conducted. [false]

2. If an event is considered to be unlikely, then although it will not occur often, the   possibility that the event could occur does exist. [true]

3. When an event is certain to occur, there is still a small chance it will not occur on   occasion. [false]

4. When an event is considered to be impossible, it will never occur as long as the   circumstances remain the same.   [true]

More Likely, Less Likely, Equally Likely

1. A spinner used for playing board games is half red and half blue. What is the   likelihood that the arrow will land in the blue area? [equally likely to land on red   or blue]

2. During the winter months in Michigan, what is the likelihood that it will snow?   [more likely in winter than other months]

3. During the hot summer months in the desert, what is the likelihood of rain? [it is   less likely to rain]

4. A bag full of jellybeans has 100 red jellybeans and 5 yellow jellybeans. Which   color is more likely to be grabbed in a handful?   [red]

5. A deck of cards has exactly 4 kings and 4 queens. If only these 8 cards are used,   what is the likelihood of drawing a king rather than a queen? {it is equally likely   to draw a king or queen]

6. A teacher hands out pencils to her class to take a test. There are forty students and 50 pencils. If only two of the pencils are sharpened, what is the likelihood that a   student will get a sharpened pencil? [it is less likely than getting a non-sharpened   pencil]

7. A tennis champion has won 9 out of the last 10 matches against his opponent. Is it more likely or less likely that he will win the next match against this same   opponent? [more likely]

8. If a second grade student reaches into a bag containing the last 10 chocolate bars   and last 3 lollipops from Halloween, which sweet treat is more likely to be   grabbed? [chocolate]

9. Mr. Smith has carved the Smith Family Thanksgiving turkey for the last 8   Thanksgiving dinners. It is more likely or less likely that he will carve the turkey   again this year?   [more likely]

10. Madison watches cartoon everyday after school for a half-hour before doing her   homework. Is it more or less likely she will do her homework before watching   cartoons tomorrow after school? [less likely]

Certain, Probable, Unlikely, Impossible

1. The sun rises in the east and sets in the west. What is the likelihood that it will   rise in the west tomorrow morning? [impossible]

2. A robin lays three eggs in the spring. What is the likelihood that all three chicks   will be baby robins? [certain]

3. A monarch caterpillar spins a cocoon and undergoes the change into a butterfly.   What is the likelihood that it will emerge as a Blue Morpho butterfly?   [impossible]

4. A bag contains 25 black checkers and 1 red checker. What is the likelihood that a black checker will be blindly chosen? [probable]

5. A dozen chocolate chip cookies are made with semi-sweet chocolate chips. What is the likelihood that there will be a cookie with white chocolate chips?   [impossible]

6. A package of cherry popsicles is purchased at the store. What is the likelihood   that when opened the package will contain grape popsicles? [impossible]

Probability – Quiz

1. Which graph shows the possibility of two event outcomes?   [Chart 1]

2. Which graph shows either a certain outcome or an impossible outcome? [Chart 2]

3. In Chart 1, which color depicts the less likely outcome? {light gray]

4. What is the likelihood of an arrow hitting a white slice on Graph 2? [impossible]

5. What is the likelihood of a paintball striking the dark gray area on Chart 1?   [probable]

6. If the light gray portion of Chart 1 was increased to cover half of the circle, would the likelihood of it being struck by a paintball increase or decrease? [increase]

7. A box of crayons contains 20 purple and 20 orange colored crayons. If a student   reaches into the box without looking into it, what is the likelihood that an orange   crayon will be chosen opposed to a purple crayon? [the likelihood is equal of   choosing a purple or orange crayon]

8. A teacher passes out a spelling test. All the students passed the pre-test given the   day before. Is it more or less likely that all of the students will pass the test.?

    [more likely]

9. A newspaper boy always throws the paper so it lands on the front porch of a   specific house. When he delivers his paper tomorrow morning, what is the   likelihood that the paper he throws lands on the front porch again?   [probable]

10. As the earth circles the sun, seasons change in certain parts of the world. The cycle is winter, spring, summer, and fall. What is the possibility that summer will follow winter next year? {impossible]

Graphs – Practice Sheet

1. What type of graph is present above?   [coordinate graph]

2. How many coordinates have been plotted? [5]

3. Which color point has the greatest vertical value?   [red]

4. Which color point has 2 even coordinates? [yellow]

5. Which color point is farthest left? [violet]

6. Which color point has the greatest horizontal coordinate? [yellow]

Based on the above graph, answer the following questions:

1. What type of graph is the graph above?   [bar graph]

2. Which eye color do most students have?   [blue]

3. How many more students have green eyes than brown?   [4]

4. How many more students have blue eyes than brown?   [8]

1. What type of graph is presented above?   [pictograph]

2. Which fruit did Sarah eat more of than the other students? [bananas]

3. Which student ate the fewest bananas? [Karie]

4. Which two fruits were consumed in equal total amounts?   [apples and oranges]

1. What type of graph is shown above?   [line plot]

2. Which fruit is most popular? [apples]

3. Which fruit is least popular? [oranges]

4. If each ✖ equals two students, how many students were polled?   [36]

1. What type of graph is presented above?   [line graph]

2. Does the graph show an increase in bag lunches over 5 days or a decrease?   [increase]

Graphs - Quiz

1. Which graph is a coordinate graph?   [Graph A]

2. Which graph is a bar graph? [Graph B]

3. Which graph is a line graph? {Graph C]

4. Which graph shows a steady increase in data over time?   [Graph C]

5. Which graph could show the square miles of water, flat land, and trees in an area   to be developed? [Graph B]

6. How many points are plotted on the coordinate graph?   [5]

7. How many data groups are used on the bar graph?   [3]

8. Which two graphs could be converted one into the other easily? [Graphs A and C]

9. Which two graphs previously discussed are missing? [pictograph and line plot]

10. True or False, graphs allow the student to visually asses a variety of data?   [true]

Second Grade Social Science
(For Homeschool or Extra Practice)

By Terri Raymond

Section 1: Family History

In our everyday lives, we can see evidence of the past. Photographs are one way of telling us what someone did years, days, or even minutes ago. But one of the easiest ways to look at the past is in your very own house: your family! Just like you, your parents or guardians were your age. They learned how to walk and talk and all about the world around them; they even learned about family history.

Just like you have a mother and father, so did *they* have a mother and father, and *they* had a mother and father, and it keeps on going back for thousands of years. Humans have been on the earth for a long time, so there's a lot of information for us to learn. We're going to start with your family, which includes how you can find out more about your family's past. In addition to that, you're going to learn more about your own life, and what the future years hold for you.

Let's begin with a basic description of the people in your family. It's likely that you have two parents, a mother and a father. Your mother has a mother, called your *grandmother*, and a father, called your *grandfather*. The same applies to your dad! Now that we have the basic idea in mind, there is something called a *family tree* that helps us to map out our ancestors. They start with you at the bottom, and then one step that leads to your mother and father above you. They each have another step that leads to *their* mother and father, and so on.

But sometimes family records are not so clear. Let's say that you have no idea who your grandparents' parents were; how in the world would you find out?

Each year, the United States government issues something called a *census.* When you fill out your census, you need to include your name, your birthday, the number of children you have, your spouse's name, and so on. Basically, it's a way for the government to keep all of our information in one safe place, and also know how many people are living in the country. When it comes to tracking down your family history, the census can be useful because you can access records that you may have had before.

But that's all. When a person is born, they are instantly given a *birth certificate*. This just proves that you were born (it also shows where you born, and what day). Some places have birth certificate records, so it's easy to find out who was in your family.

There is an entire field of study called *genealogy*, or the study of tracing ancestors. In today's modern, digital world, there are entire websites devotes to finding out more about your family history. In fact, today, people can share information across the Internet that can put you in touch with family you never even knew you had! People who do genealogy for a living are called *genealogists*. While they do help common people discover more about their family history, they also try to figure out the family lines of celebrities and even British kings. It's a very interesting line of work!

Newspapers print obituaries as well; when a person dies, a small comment about their life is included in the paper. Genealogists will often search for obituary records to discover more about the death of a person.

There are plenty of other ways to find out more information about your ancestors, such as letters or papers they may have left behind; a will that they wrote before they died; or even their license of marriage. With permission from your parents, you could probably check out some of these cool items!

So now that we have learned a bunch of cool ways to figure out the past, we can organize these sources into two different categories. The first category is called a primary source, and the second is called a secondary source.

Primary means first, or something that is main and central. A difference between a primary and a secondary source is best explained through the following example: During World War II, a young girl named Anne Frank hid from enemy soldiers. She wrote about her experiences in a book called *The Diary of Anne Frank*. This is considered a primary source because Anne Frank was there and experienced her story. Later, many people wrote essays and articles, and even books, about her life. Those essays are considered secondary sources, because they were *about* the primary source.

Another example: Many archaeologists discovered Native American pottery, centuries old. These artifacts are primary sources because they are directly from the time period. If someone then wrote an essay about Native American pottery, that essay would be a secondary source.

Can you think of any other secondary sources? Well, you're reading one! This curriculum relays historical information to you, the reader, even though the author wasn't actually there.

Here is a list of primary and secondary sources.

Primary: journals (*The Diary of Anne Frank*), historical documents (The Declaration of Independence), artifacts (tools, clothing, or anything else from the past).

Secondary: Books written about history, essays, textbooks, and so on.

Let's say, for example, that you wanted to look into the life of your grandfather. You find a letter that he wrote years ago; this is a primary source. Then you find a picture that he painted when he was a young boy; this is a secondary source. Both of them can tell you something about his life, but they are different types of sources.

Since we live in the United States of America, our ancestors may only have been here for a few hundred years or less (unless you have a Native American background, in which case your ancestors have been here for a long time!). The Americas were discovered in the 1400s by European explorers, who then brought people over to populate these lands. Most of the people in the United States have ancestors that arrived from Europe centuries ago, but more people continue to come to America each day.

Since people are constantly moving in and out of countries, there are two important terms to know before we continue.

The first term is *emigration*, which is what you do when you *leave* a country. For example, people that went to the New World (America) emigrated from European countries. If you leave America and move somewhere else, you emigrate from America.

The second term is *immigration*, which what you do when *enter* a country. For example, people that left Europe *immigrated* to the New World. If your family decided to move to Japan, you will be *immigrating* to Japan. The word *immigration* is a very important word to know, because it is one of the main problems that the United States government faces today. In recent years, thousands of people from Mexico and Central America have been trying to immigrate into the United States, some of them legally and some of them illegally. If you want to understand the modern United States, then *immigration* is a word you definitely have to know!

It is important to understand these terms because the world is constantly changing; people are moving, and that will affect your children, your children's children, and your children's children's children! Have you moved anywhere during your life?

Long ago, no one lived in America—not even the Native Americans, who descended from Asians that crossed a strip of land called the Bering Strait. The Bering Strait connected Russia and Alaska. Eventually the humans populated what we know to today as Canada and the United States, Mexico, Central America, and all of South America. Essentially, Native Americans have common ancestry in the humans that came from Asia.

America, though, is full of rich cultures that have arrived from all over the world, from every country. If you look at the average classroom today, you will see many ethnicities and races that have traveled generations to arrive there. You can look back at your line ancestry, see what countries your ancestors are from—did they have the same religion as you? Same skin color?

Ancestry is a great thing to explore. It can tell you a lot about your family, but even more than that, it can tell you a lot about yourself. Knowing your origins is very special, and in our modern age of advanced technology, we have excellent ways of doing so. We should not take these methods for granted; on the Internet, there are numerous websites devoted to tracing lineage through documents and records. You can trace your family and learn all about your past, and it might bring some things to light about your family that you never knew before. For example, did you know that Abraham Lincoln is the half-first cousin five times removed of actor George Clooney? The more you know!

Related to ancestry, timelines are a great way to study the past. Timelines depict events in the order that they happened. When things are in this order, this is called *chronological order*. Timelines put things in perspective: we can see what happened and when, and in relation to other events. Timelines are often used in history to study important events. You can create timelines in a number of ways.

First, you can create a vertical timeline. Think of a piece of paper with a line drawn the middle. Your first event will be written at the very top, on the left side. Your second event will sit below that, on the right side. Third, on the left, fourth, on the right, and down and down until you hit the bottom.

Second, you can create a horizontal timeline. It is the same idea as the other timeline, except you will tilt your piece of paper the other way. Draw a line across the paper, from left to right. Your first event will be on the left at the top, second on the bottom, third on the top, fourth on the bottom, and on and on until hit the right side of the page.

So now that you know what types of timelines there are, we will explore what events you can put on a timeline of your own life. First, obviously, is your birthday! You would want to include your birthday as the first event in your life. Some other cool ideas for important events in your life are listed below:

- Your first word

- Your first haircut

- The first time you walked

- Your first day of school

You can choose from other events, such as playing sports, the birth of a sibling, vacations that you have been on, and anything else that you can think of. If you have enough space, you can write a short blurb about each event. You do not have to do this now; it will be included in your Activities section. Just keep in mind what makes each of these events significant; why are they important in your life? What do they mean to you? How might you remember them in the future? Did your friends have similar events, or are you the only one? Did your parents, guardians, or grandparents have similar events happen to them during the course of their life?

With each event, you'll probably want to include the date. A date consists of the month number, the day number, and the year number. For example, if someone was born on June 21, 1994, his or her birthdate would be written as 6-21-94. Often, you abbreviate the year number to the final two digits.

But why is this important? Why would you want to organize these important in your life? First of all, it's crucial to recognize what events in your life are significant. It's nice to know what day you were born, and in what order things have happened in your life. You can always add onto your timeline as more important things happen to you, or things that you would like to remember. Especially today, *time* is a very important idea. We use calendars to keep dates and appointments, we use watches and cell phones to look at the clock and keep the time. As you get older, time will become more and more relevant to your everyday life—and not just the minutes and hours of the day, but the years and important events that happened. Keeping your timeline will help you keep track of all these events, and keep them in order.

It would be a good idea to talk to your parents, your guardians, or your grandparents about their lives too. Perhaps you can even create timelines for their lives. If they cannot remember specific dates, that's okay—but organizing a precise chronology of events if very important. You can get more ideas from them, and know what cool first events may be in store for you.

If you are take any major lessons away from this, it would be a beginning idea of how time works, and understanding that things happened in the past that can connect to how you live today. Through your own research, you can explore what happened to your parents/guardians, your grandparents, and even further back in your family lineage. Another lesson to learn would be how to create a proper timeline, and how you might use one in your everyday life—such as planning out your daily schedule.

Just like you, your ancestors—even as immediate as your parents—value a set of dates and important events that make up the chronology of their life: their birthday, their first day of school, their first relationships, the day they were accepted into college and left home, and so on. It is important for you to keep all of this in perspective.

But timelines and ancestry are not just for personal use. They are also used heavily by historians all the time! One common example is in the study of the American Civil War, a period of time in which the northern states battled the southern states. It was the first American war in which photographs were abundantly used, so historians have a lot of visual, photographic records of the soldiers that fought. These photographs, and the notes and records that accompany them, can be used to trace ancestry—we can tell what people today have ancestors that fought in the Civil War.

Using diaries and letters, *primary sources*, we can create a timeline, or a *chronology* of a person's life. Think about each piece of information as a puzzle piece, and getting more knowledge will fill out the larger picture. This is how historians feel when they do research and try to identify each artifact from the past.

More than just the ancestry of celebrities and famous historical figures, historians have lately been examining the family trees and ancestry of the common people. They have realized that learning more about the common people will reveal a greater picture than just the famous celebrities of the time. You can tell what individual life was like through these artifacts, and learn a lot about the past.

Learning about someone else's life can help you learn about yours. Do you have ancestors that fought in the Civil War? Did they come from another country? What was their history in that country? Did they believe in a different religion? Did they fight in any wars? Why did they come to America? When did they come to America? Why are you living where you are now? What changes in your ancestry may have affected your current life, and how can this knowledge help you better understand who you are today? Ancestry is not just what happened to your ancestors, but also their *genetics*, or what makes up our bodies and decides what we look like and sometimes who we are. If you have blond hair, do all of you ancestors have blond hair? What might have changed your hair color along the line? These are all great questions that you can seek answers to as you explore your own ancestry. Perhaps it will give you a new view on your history!

Today, your life may drastically differ from that of your ancestors. In an age where technology is rapidly expanding, you have access to countless resources that people never had before: cell phones, computers, immense databases. With a single phone in your pocket, you can retrieve treasure troves of information from around the world. At this moment in time, humans have higher access to knowledge than any other humans before us. Essentially, we should take advantage of these great opportunities. This is one way in which your life might differ from that of your parents/guardians, or grandparents. Did they use computers growing up? What kind were they? Did they use the library more than the computer? What did they do for fun? These are just some things that you can think about as you wonder how your ancestors' lives were different from your own.

Humans have been around for generations, and each of these generations has countless stories to tell us. Your generation, especially you, will have stories to tell. As you study what happened in the past, you will be more prepared to face the present and ready for the future. Comparing your life to others is a great tool, as well as organizing your life into a series of chronological events. As you go forward with this information, keep an open mind, be prepared to learn new things, and be ready to have creative and practical discussions about the lives of your ancestors, your parents/guardians, and your own life: where it has been, and where it is going. This will be an adequate preparation for you in the years to come, as you grow up, mature, and become an integral part to human society.

Discussion Questions

(1) What does the word "ancestry" mean? Can you use the word in a sentence, and might it mean different things to different people?

(2) What is the difference between a primary and secondary source? Do you think one of them is more valuable and better to look at? What are the advantages/disadvantages of having a primary source? What are the advantages/disadvantages of having a secondary source?

(3) What are some ways in which you can trace your family history? Are there any methods that are clearly better than the others? How and why?

(4) Why is having a *census* each year important? What would happen if we did not have a census? Would it be good or bad?

(5) What is the difference between immigration and emigration? What effects do they have on the world today? Was there any immigration/emigration in your family's ancestral history?

(6) How were the Americas populated? Did this affect your own history at all? Why or why not?

(7) Why is a timeline useful? Why should you create one in order to learn more? Are there any reasons why timelines are not helpful?

(8) What are some important events that you might like to put on your timelines? Discuss some ideas, and keep them in mind for the Activities section.

(9) In what ways is your life different from that of your ancestors? From your parents?

(10) How can studying the past help you understand the present?

Activities

(1) Watch the following video about researching your family history. You may use the helpful tips in this video as you further explore your history in the future activities: https://www.youtube.com/watch?v=xr6y_Lv6MQ8.

(2) With help from your family, find any documents, records, artifacts, or photographs in your house that might be useful in determining who your ancestors were and what they were like. For each piece of evidence, write a single sentence about how that helps you learn about your family history.

(3) Create a list of all the different family members that you have: parents, grandparents, cousins, siblings, uncles, aunts, and any others that you want to include. Write down their names, and get started on your very own family tree. You can choose how far back you want to research. You can find templates for family trees online, or just draw your own!

(4) Create a chart on a piece of paper, with two columns. The first column is "Primary Sources," and the second is "secondary sources." Come up with ten examples for each column; you may use the library or the Internet to find ideas.

(5) If you have ancestors that immigrated to the New World, imagine that you are one of them any write a one-page journal entry from their point-of-view. If you have ancestors that are Native Americans, imagine that you are living in the New World before any Europeans arrived. If you are not sure, you can pick one of the two options. Feel free to be creative and have fun!

(6) Find a map of America that includes the Bering Strait, connecting Alaska and Russia. Color North America blue, Central America red, and South America green. Draw arrows leading from Russia to the Americas, down to Central and South America. This will help you understand how far humans traveled when they arrived in the Americas!

(7) Compare and contrast you and your ancestors! Create a Venn diagram. One circle will be your ancestors that lived before you, and the other circle will be you. How is your life different? How is your life similar? Do you face the same challenges?

(8) Create a timeline of your life! You may choose a vertical or horizontal timeline, as well as what dates *you* think are important enough to include. Make sure to include dates, as well as *why* each event is important to your life.

(9) Imagine you are a historian researching the American Civil War. You've just found a very important artifact (it can be whatever you choose: letter, photograph, weapon, etc.), and you are writing to a friend about why this artifact is so important, and why it might help you understand someone's family history.

(10) Think about something that you will leave behind that will help your future generations understand your life: a document? A letter? A favorite object, such as a toy or something valuable? Write a paragraph about how it might help people understand you and your life.

For Further Reading

Beller, Susan Provost. *Roots for Kids: A Genealogy Guide for Young People.* Genealogical Publishing Company, 2010.

Chorzempa, Rosemary. *My Family Tree Workbook: Genealogy for Beginners.* Dover Publications, 1982.

Cooper, J. California. Doubleday, 1990.

Dennen, Karen Frisch. *Creating Junior Genealogists: Tips and Activities for Family History Fun.* Turner, 2003.

Gibson, Karen Bush. *Native American History for Kids, with 21 Activities.* Chicago Review Press, 2010.

Hickey, M. Gail. *Bringing History Home: Local and Family History Projects for Grades K-6.* Pearson Education, 1998.

Lang, Suzanne. *Families, Families, Families!* Random House, 2015.

Lark, Ronni Lundy. *Conversations with My Mother: A Keepsake Journal for Celebrating a Lifetime of Stories.* Lark Crafts, 2007.

Leavitt, Caroline. *The Kids' Family Tree Book.* Sterling, 2007.

Maloof, Karen. *For My Grandchild: An Album of Memories from grandparent to Grandchild.* Ideals Publications, 1994.

Parr, Todd. *The Family Book.* Little Brown Books for Young Readers, 2010.

Orr, Tamra. *How to Research Your Ancestry.* Mitchell Lane Publishers, 2011.

Sauncers-Smith, Gail. *Families.* Capstone Press, 1997.

Wolfman, Ira. *Climbing Your Family Tree: Online and Off-Line Genealogy for Kids.* Workman, 2001.

Wolfman, Ira. *Do People Grow on Family Trees? Genealogy for Kids and Other Beginners.* Workman, 1991.

Quiz

(1) Which of the following is not a method of tracing ancestry?
    (A) Family trees
    (B) Second-guessing
    (C) Photographs
    (D) Letters

(2) Each year, the United States government issues a _____ that keeps tracks of names, dates, addresses, and other important information.
    (A) Evidence warrant
    (B) Census
    (C) Food survey
    (D) Multiple choice questionnaire

(3) What is genealogy?
    (A) The study of your cousins
    (B) The study of ancestry
    (C) The study of primary source documents
    (D) The study of secondary source documents

(4) Which of the following is NOT a primary source?
    (A) A letter written by your grandfather
    (B) A photograph from the 1800s
    (C) A textbook about the American Revolution, written two years ago
    (D) A bowl that Native Americans used to eat

(5) Which of the following is NOT a secondary source?
    (A) A textbook about Chinese history
    (B) A novel written about fictional characters during World War II
    (C) A painting that someone drew in 2005 of George Washington in 1776
    (D) A letter written by President Abraham Lincoln

(6) Many Europeans _____ *from* Europe.

(A) Immigrated

(B) Emigrated

(7) Many Europeans _____ *to* the New World.
  (A) Immigrated
  (B) Emigrated

(8) What once connected Alaska and Russia?
  (A) The Bering Strait
  (B) The Narrow Sea
  (C) The Strait of Gibraltar
  (D) The Russo-Alaskan Strait

(9) The first humans to settle in the Americas came from what continent?
  (A) Europe
  (B) South America
  (C) Australia
  (D) Asia

(10) Which of the following is NOT a type of timeline that you learned about?
  (A) Vertical
  (B) Horizontal
  (C) Diagonal
  (D) None of the above

(11) How would June 21st, 1994 be written in an abbreviated date?
  (A) 1994-6-21
  (B) 21-6-94
  (C) 6-21-94
  (D) 94-21-6

(12) Which of the following does the government give you when you are born?
  (A) A birthmark
  (B) A birth certificate
  (C) A gift certificate to a baby store
  (D) A family tree

(13) Who lived in the Americas before the Europeans arrived?
  (A) Indians
  (B) Native Americans
  (C) Arcticmen
  (D) Vikings

(14) Which of the following do you have today that your ancestors a hundred years ago did not have?
  (A) Paper
  (B) Cellular phones
  (C) Cameras

(D) Trains

(15) If events are placed in the order that they happened, then they are in _____ order.
    (A) Chronological
    (B) Primary
    (C) Secondary
    (D) Organized

(16) Obituaries are written about someone in the newspaper if they have died.
    (A) True
    (B) False

(17) Historians use family trees.
    (A) True
    (B) False

(18) Obituary is the study of ancestry.
    (A) True
    (B) False

(19) Learning from the past can help us prepare for the future.
    (A) True
    (B) False

(20) There was once a time when North, Central, and South America were completely uninhabited.
    (A) True
    (B) False

Quiz Answers

1. **B.** Second-guessing is not a method of tracing ancestry.
2. **B.** Each year, the U.S. government issues a census.
3. **B.** Genealogy is the study of ancestry.
4. **C.** A textbook is not a primary source.
5. **D.** An official letter is not a secondary source.
6. **B.** Many Europeans emigrated *from* Europe.
7. **A.** Many Europeans immigrated *to* the New World.
8. **A.** The Bering Straight once connected Alaska and Russia
9. **D.** The first humans to settle in the Americas came from Asia.
10. **C.** We did not learn about diagonal timelines.
11. **C.** June 21st, 1994 would be written as 6-21-94.
12. **B.** The government gives you a birth certificate when you are born.
13. **B.** Native Americans lived in the Americas before Europeans arrived.
14. **B.** Our ancestors a hundred years ago did not have cell phones.
15. **A.** If events are placed in the order that they happened, they are in chronological order.
16. **True.** Obituaries are written in the paper if someone dies.
17. **True.** Historians use family trees for research.
18. **False.** Genealogy is the study of ancestry.
19. **True.** Learning from the past can help us prepare for the future.
20. **True.** There was a time when North, Central, and South America were completely uninhabited.

Section 2: Maps

You have probably heard the word before, and maybe even used one: *map*. People use maps every single day to find out where they are going, where they have been, and where they plan to go in the future. Historians use maps to solve the mysteries of the past, and many use maps in order to trade goods with other people. Maps are a great way for people to orient themselves in the world. A map can tell you exactly where you live – in your neighborhood, in your city, in your state, in your country, in your continent, in the world!

Maps have been used for hundreds of years, and they have come a very long way. While before maps were primitive and not very exact, today we have satellites that circle the earth that chart land for us. GPS is available on your phone—it stands for Global Positioning System, and it can tell you how to get from one place to another.

But more than tell you where you are living right now, maps can tell you where your ancestors lived. We will get into that later; first, we are going to explore the aspects of a map: how to read one, how to use one efficiently, and what maps can do for you. We will also look at the different areas of cities and towns, and how maps demonstrate those.

Let us begin with the word *geography*. "Geo" means "earth," and "graphy" means that it is a descriptive science. Loosely, it means "earth description," and it is the science of maps, and of the earth itself. Geographers mainly study different types of land and geographical features such as mountains, valleys, or rivers. It the study of how amazing Earth can be, and making sense of it all.

A map is any picture or drawing of an area that uses words and symbols to tell you what's there. You have probably seen a map of the world before: it shows all seven continents, the name of countries and oceans, rivers and mountain ranges, and other important features.

There are seven different continents: North America (where you live!), South America, Europe, Africa, Asia, Australia, and Antarctica. Five of the seven continents have other countries in them, while Australia and Antarctica are technically their own countries.

There are five major oceans: the Arctic Ocean, the Pacific Ocean, the Atlantic Ocean, the Indian Ocean, and the Antarctic Ocean. It is hard to compare maps to the actual space of the earth; while most maps are printed on a flat piece of rectangular paper, the earth is a sphere, a perfect ball. Because of this, maps will often misconstrue the actual sizes of certain continents and countries. Today, many researchers are understanding that Africa has long been represented as much smaller than it actually is. Even if maps are not perfect, however, they are useful in seeing where you are in comparison to the rest of the world, or where other people have been.

There are two different types of maps:

Political Map – A political map shows boundaries between states and countries. It is used mainly to show cities, capitals, and names. It will also show the names of rivers and bodies of water.

Physical Map – A physical map shows the characteristics of the land. It will focus more on terrain, such as mountains, deserts, plains, and rivers.

Both political and physical maps have their advantages. If you wanted to trace your family, you would likely be interested in a political map so you can see the cities and towns where your ancestors may have lived, rather than features of the land. During your studies, you may find need for both. Just remember that they each have their unique purposes!

When you look at a map, you may see horizontal and vertical lines running across it. These lines are called *longitude* and *latitude*, and they are used to measure the earth. In fact, most Global Positioning Systems work with these lines and pinpoint coordinates.

Now that you know what maps can do, we look at the different parts of a map so that you're prepared to read one and understand it fully.

Title – Each map has a title. While this may seem like something that you can easily skip over, take some time to look at the title so that you know what the map is about before you even look at it.

Scale – Maps have the tough job of measuring thousands of miles on just a few inches of paper. Usually, maps will have a rule, such as 'one inch equals a certain number of miles.' You can use this to measure length and distance between places, and understand how big places are.

Compass: A compass shows you which way is north, just in case the map is tilted and slightly off. The compass will point in four directions: North, East, South, and West. You can use these four directions to see where things are in relation to each other. For example, if you were comparing California and Arizona, you might say that California is west of Arizona.

Key: Map keys will usually give you symbols that tell you what is on the map. For example, a small black dot represents a city, while a large black dot represents a major city, while a star represents a capital. It is always wise to look at the key before you look at the map; that way, you know what you are looking for and what symbols on the map will mean.

When we look at the United States, we can see that the country is made of different regions: the northeast, southeast, midwest, west, and southwest. Each of these regions is made of several states. Each state is made of different counties, and each country is made of different cities and towns. Each city and town has many neighborhoods, and each neighborhood is made of streets and houses.

Different areas of towns and cities are broken up into three different categorizations that describe them: rural, suburban, and urban. We will begin with a description of a rural environment.

Rural: In this type of area, there will be a lot of open space. The land will likely contain rolling hills, farms, fields, and is not generally an area where many people live. Rural areas are where many fruits and vegetables are produced; the wide, open space is great for plentiful vegetation.

Suburban: Suburban areas are more populated than rural areas, but less populated than urban areas. Suburban areas will have neighborhoods, some with apartments, many with houses. There will shops, parks, sidewalks, and other nice commodities in suburban neighborhoods.

Urban: An urban neighborhood is a city. There will be buildings, and perhaps even skyscrapers. Businesses will be everywhere, and there will likely be more apartments than houses, with lots of people. Urban areas are the most populated areas.

Maps can cover anything: a single neighborhood, a city, a county, state, region, country, or the world. On any map that you see, you might find different features. We already talked about some features: oceans, rivers, cities, mountains, and so on. Now we are going to organize these features into two different categories.

Cultural Features: These are things that have been created by mankind. These include towns and cities, and especially borders. Lines on a map are used to define territory. These borders change over time, so it is especially interesting for historians and geographers to look at how maps have changed over time. Sometimes, people argue and fight over borders. If this is the case, then people who make maps (*cartographers*) will use a dotted line instead of a solid line to show that the border is not yet decided.

When cartographers draw their maps, they have to deal with how to type the names of cities, states, and countries. Because countries are bigger, they will usually write the name of the country in big capital letters, while everything else is lowercase.

Physical Features: These are things that are natural and have not been created by mankind. There are certain lines called *contour lines* that show the height of things like mountains. They usually only exist on physical maps; they are drawn around the mountain and get smaller as you get closer to the peak. They will usually have the number of feet around each contour line, to show how high the mountain is at that point. On a political map, it is rare to find contour lines. They help people find out the elevation of a mountain, find the height of cliffs, and *plateaus*. A plateau is a sudden, heightened piece of land.

The point of physical features is to show what the land looks like. These features can often be found in the key of the map, like mountains, valleys, and rivers.

Now that you know all of the key assets of a map, you will soon be ready to explore and interpret maps for yourselves. One of the greatest things you can do with your map-reading abilities is plot out where your ancestors have lived in the past. This will be an excellent addition to your previous studies of your family history.

Perhaps your ancestors came from another country; but for many of you, your ancestors have moved around the United States quite a bit, from neighborhoods and towns and states. To get a better comprehension of United States geography, we will be going through all of the most significant United States features.

First, we will return to the different regions of the United States. Here is a list of each region and the states that it includes, along with some geographic information:

Northeast: Maine, New Hampshire, Massachusetts, Rhode Island, Connecticut, Vermont, New York, Pennsylvania, New Jersey, Delaware, Maryland.

It is in the Northeast that we see the northern end of the Appalachian Mountains, which stretch into the south. They reach into Pennsylvania. Bordering the northeastern region is the Atlantic Ocean, always painted blue or white on maps. Also bordering the northeast are some of the Great Lakes, which are also near the midwest region.

Midwest: North Dakota, South Dakota, Nebraska, Iowa, Kansas, Ohio, Indiana, Michigan, Illinois, Missouri, Wisconsin, and Minnesota.

The Midwest states also the Great Lakes, which we will explore more later. The Midwest has a lot of open land, and a lot of this is called the Great Plains. They are vast and home to abundant wildlife, such as the buffalo. The Great Plains is a popular destination spot, especially for their beautiful scenery.

Southeast: Florida, Louisiana, Mississippi, Alabama, Georgia, North Carolina, South Carolina, Tennessee, Kentucky, Virginia, West Virginia

The Southeastern states are home to the rest of the Appalachian Mountains, and also the famous Smoky Mountains of Tennessee. These are both popular areas for tourists to hike and travel. The forests there span thousands of acres. As for the oceans they border, the Southeast touches both the Atlantic Ocean in the east and the Gulf of Mexico in the south. Along its western states meanders the rest of the Mississippi River, which begins in the Midwest.

West: California, Nevada, Utah, Wyoming, Idaho, Montana, Oregon, Alaska, Hawaii

The west is known for its incredible scenery, in both national parks and natural landmarks. There are two mountain ranges, the Sierras and the Rocky Mountains. But even if you can find the tallest American mountains out west, you can also find the vastest deserts. The Mojave Desert sits in the western region. The west borders the Pacific Ocean. As for its land borders, you can find Canada to the north and Mexico to the south.

Southwest: Arizona, New Mexico, Oklahoma, Texas

In the southwest you can also find a continuation of the Rocky Mountains. Also in this region you can find one of the most visited tourist spots in the world: the Grand Canyon, which many people call the most beautiful place in the world. You can also find the Colorado River here, one of the longest rivers in the United States.

In terms of rivers, the United States is plentiful with them. The Missouri River is the longest river in the United States; it begins in Montana and snakes all the way to St. Louis, Missouri. It was often used by Native Americans, but the first Europeans who found it were the famous explorers Lewis and Clark.

The Mississippi River begins in Minnesota and ends when it travels through Louisiana and filters into the Gulf of Mexico. The Yukon River actually begins in Canada but winds through Alaska and empties into the Bering Sea on the coast of western Alaska.

The United States is also home to some of the most amazing lakes in the world. Foremost among them are the five Great Lakes in the north. There is Lake Huron, Lake Ontario, Lake Michigan, Lake Erie, and Lake Superior. Together, the initials of their names spell "H.O.M.E.S.," which is a good way to remember their names. They are shared territory with Canada (except for Lake Michigan, which entirely belongs to the United States).

If you ever travel across the United States of America, you will surely see a variety of mountain ranges that are renowned across the world as some of the most beautiful and scenic places to visit. Beginning in the east, there are the lovely Appalachian Mountains. They stretch for 1500 miles, from Maine all the way down to Alabama. The Appalachians are abundant with both flora and fauna (plants and animals); some of the animals include bears, wolves, deer, beavers, and others. Many people have tried and succeeded to hike the entire length of the Appalachian Trail, which takes months to accomplish (imagine the amount of walking you have to do, and the supplies you have to carry!).

In early American history, settlers used the Appalachian Mountains as a border—the settlers were not allowed to travel beyond these mountains, which was seen as dangerous Native American land. Eventually, however, Europeans did push beyond the Appalachians, resulting in widespread destruction and massacres of Native Americans.

If you've ever heard of the Smoky Mountains of Tennessee, they are a small part of the larger Appalachian Mountain range, along with the White Mountains of New Hampshire and the Berkshire Mountains of Massachusetts.

Out west, the Rocky Mountains stand as the second-longest mountain range in the world, and the first in North America. They run for 3,000 miles, from Canada to New Mexico. Like the Appalachians, the Rocky Mountains are home to an abundance of wild life, from bears to bighorn sheep to deer to elk, and even coyotes. It is within the Rocky Mountains that something called the "Continental Divide" is located.

Most fresh water sources come from the top of a mountain; the water flows down and deposits into a river. Many of these rivers lead to lakes, and others flow all the way to the ocean. In the Rocky Mountains, there are many rivers that diverge. One meanders east to the Atlantic Ocean, and the other snakes west to the Pacific Ocean. This shows how important the Rocky Mountains are to our rivers all across the United States!

The Rocky Mountains are also home to some of the world's most treasured national parks, values both because of their wildlife and because their unrivaled scenic vistas. These parks include Glacier National Park in Montana, Yellowstone and Grand Teton National Parks in Wyoming, and Rocky Mountain National Park in Colorado. These areas are protected from people that want to build houses or cut down trees, in order to save what animals and plants remain there. Hopefully, these wonderful parks will always be protected.

The final important mountain range in the United States is the Sierra Nevada. It exists mostly in California (and a little bit of Nevada), stretching four hundred miles. While it may not live up to the length of the Appalachians or the Rockies, it is home to the tallest and largest trees in the world. They are called sequoia trees, and a single tree can stretch to 270 feet high, and 25 feet across. Scientists and conservationists are continually protecting these trees from being cut down, especially because they believe that some of them are over three thousand years old, having survived too long a time to be cut down by humans.

The Sierra Nevada Mountains are home to the glorious Yosemite National Park, which has been subject to poems and songs abounding. One particular song is "Yosemite Autumn," a piece written by composer Mark Camphouse (more on this in the Activities section!).

Finally, we will explore the United States deserts. The largest desert in the country is the Great Basin Desert, which covers areas between the Rocky Mountains and the Sierra Nevada. It exists in Oregon, Idaho, California, and Utah. Unlike many deserts, it is not hot—in fact, it is cold, snowy, and dry.

The Mojave Desert rests below the Great Basin, stretching across California, Arizona, and Nevada. During the day, the temperatures are scorching hot, while at night they are freezing. The Mojave is home to a place called Death Valley, appropriately named because of how dangerous it can be.

The Sonoran Desert lies below the Mojave, wresting in California, Arizona, and parts of northern Mexico. The Colorado River flows threw the Sonoran, one of the main supplies of water in the region. When you think of a cactus in a desert, you are likely imagining the saguaro cactus that calls the Sonoran Desert its home.

The final big desert is the Chihuahuan Desert, which exists mostly in Mexico but does stretch into Arizona, New Mexico, and Texas. It is home to the Rio Grande River, which meanders through the desert and then deposits into the Gulf of Mexico in the east. In the desert you can also find Big Bend National Park, whose purpose is to save and protect the wildlife and the vegetation.

Hopefully this has given you a comprehensive overview of both maps and United States geography. With this information, you can explore how maps function and their usefulness to us today. They are an excellent tool, and will aid you in your education and your life. You can now map out where you have lived, and are better equipped to explore your own family history.

Discussion Questions

(1) Do you think life is easier if we have maps on our cell phones? Should we just use paper maps? Should we still make paper maps if we have cell phones?

(2) What is the difference between a political map and a physical map? What are the advantages of having a political map? What are the advantages of having a physical map? Are there any cons?

(3) Why do we use longitude and latitude? How do they help us find locations? How are they used on maps?

(4) What is the purpose of a *scale* on a map? Why is having one important? What would happen if you did not have a scale?

(5) What is the purpose of a *key* on a map? Why is having one important? What would happen if you did not have a key?

(6) What is the difference between rural, suburban, and urban? Which type of area do you live in? Have you ever visited areas that are the other two?

(7) What is cartography? What does a cartographer do?

(8) "H.O.M.E.S." is a good way to remember the names for the Great Lakes. Why do you think this is helpful? Does it help you remember?

(9) What is the difference between cultural features and physical features? Which ones would you see a political map? Which ones would you see on a physical map?

(10) How might you use your knowledge of maps and ancestry to trace where your ancestors lived? What tools would you use?

Activities

(1) Create a Venn diagram – one circle will be Political Map/Cultural Features, and the other will be Physical Map/Physical Features.

(2) Print out *two* maps of your state. Label one a *political* map, and one of them a *physical* map. On another piece of paper, write down what things go onto each type of map. Then, first work on the political map. You will want to include important cities, borders, your state capital, and don't forget to include your city! On the physical map, include mountains, rivers, deserts, and any other physical features you find important. Feel free to make it colorful! Make your maps have a key, a scale, and any of the other important map features that we discussed.

(3) Create a Venn diagram – one circle will be Political Map/Cultural Features, and the other will be Physical Map/Physical Features. Compare and contrast!

(4) Listen to the following song, *Yosemite Autumn* composed by Mark Camphouse. It is a concert piece that captures the grandeur, beauty, and excitement of Yosemite National Park. After listening to the piece, write a short paragraph about how the song makes you feel—does it make you think of the beautiful scenic vistas of Yosemite National Park? Is there a relationship between songs and physical places? Does Mark Camphouse do a good job of capturing the idea of Yosemite?
https://www.youtube.com/watch?v=9TdS-_uOduQ

(5) Print out a blank map of the United States. This will be your political map; include all of the states, the capitals, and major cities. Use a colored pencil/crayon/marker to color in the different regions of the United States that we discussed.

(6) Print out a second blank map of the United States. This will be your physical map; include all of the rivers, mountains, deserts, and other physical features that we discussed. You may use different colors for each type of feature, if you like. Just make sure that you clearly label each one!

(7) Interview your parents/guardians about where you have lived in the past, and if they know of any places that your ancestors lived. This may be in your state, your country, or across the world. Write all of these places down, and then locate them on a map. If you can, write down the approximate years that your ancestors/parents/guardians moved and create a timeline.

(8) Print out a blank map of the world, the country, or your state. This will serve as the map that will trace the movements of your ancestors. Use arrows to trace them from place to place.

(9) Watch the following video about the "Five Themes of Geography." When you have finished, list each theme and describe why it is important to an understanding of geography. Then, write about whether this video was helpful or not to your understanding of maps.
https://www.youtube.com/watch?v=Mwkqgb4EHuA

(10) Watch the following video about maps for kids. Now that you know all about maps and geography, you will be the judge of this video: Does it do a good job teaching about maps? What does it do well? What could it do better? You be the judge! https://www.youtube.com/watch?v=FKk7tKjoLok

For Further Reading

Block, Marta Segal. *Reading Maps.* Heinemann, 2008.

Boothroyd, Jennifer. *Map My Neighborhood.* Lerner Publishing Group, 2013.

Carlisle, Madelyn Wood. *Let's Investigate Marvelously Meaningful Maps.* Barrons Juveniles, 1992.

Foster, Karen. *Kids' World Atlas: A Young Person's Guide to the Globe.* Picture Window Books, 2010.

Green, Jen. *Barron's Amazing Fact-Packed, Fold-Out Atlas of the World: With Awesome Pop-Up Map!* Barron's Educational Series, 2014.

Jaeggi, Chris. *I Know About Maps.* Rand McNally, 1995.

Knowlton, Jack. *Geography from A to Z: A Picture Glossary.* HarperCollins, 1997.

Knowlton, Jack. *Maps & Globes.* Ty Crowell Co, 1985.

Mizielinska, Aleksandra. *Maps.* Big Picture Press, 2013.

Mizielinska, Aleksandra. *Maps Activity Book.* Templar Publishing, 2014.

National Geographic. *National Geographic Kids: United States Atlas.* National Geographic Kids, 2012.

Rabe, Tish. *There's a Map on My Lap!* Random House Books, 2002.

Sweeney, Joan. *Me on the Map.* Knopf Books for Young Readers, 1996.

Taylor, Barbara. *Maps and Mapping.* Kingfisher, 1995.

Wittels, Harriet. *A Bird's Eye View: A First Book of Maps.* Scholastic Trade, 1995.

Quiz

(1) What does "geography" translate to?
  (A) "Map study"
  (B) "Earth description"
  (C) "Culture study"
  (D) "Earth maps"

(2) The following feature on a map helps the reader measure distances, comparing the length on the paper to actual distance:
  (A) Title
  (B) Key
  (C) Scale
  (D) Compass

(3) The following feature on a map helps the reader identify markers on the map, such as mountains, rivers, buildings, and so on:
  (A) Title
  (B) Key
  (C) Scale
  (D) Compass

(4) The following feature on a map helps the reader identify which direction is North, East, West, and South:
  (A) Title
  (B) Key
  (C) Scale
  (D) Compass

(5) What kind of map displays mountains, rivers, deserts, and physical features?
  (A) Political map
  (B) Physical map
  (C) Cultural map
  (D) All of the above

(6) What kind of map displays city names, country borders, and cultural features?
  (A) Political map
  (B) Physical map
  (C) Cultural map
  (D) None of the above

(7) "H.O.M.E.S." can help you remember the initials for what group of features?
  (A) The Great Deserts
  (B) The Great Lakes
  (C) The Appalachian Mountains
  (D) The Sierra Nevada Mountains

(8) Which of the following is NOT one of the five major oceans?

(A) Indian Ocean
(B) Pacific Ocean
(C) Atlantic Ocean
(D) South American Ocean

(9) Which of the following is NOT a region of the United States?
(A) Northeast
(B) West
(C) Midwest
(D) Midsouth

(10) An area that is composed of mostly farmland and not many houses or communities would be seen as:
(A) Rural
(B) Suburban
(C) Urban
(D) Urban-rural

(11) An area that is composed mostly of tall buildings, apartments, and is tight on space would be seen as:
(A) Rural
(B) Suburban
(C) Urban
(D) Subrural

(12) An area that is not too overpopulated and not too underpopulated, with a good mix of community and businesses, would be seen as:
(A) Rural
(B) Suburban
(C) Urban
(D) None of the above

(13) In early American history, what mountain range served as a border that told settlers not to go further west?
(A) Rocky Mountains
(B) Appalachian Mountains
(C) Sierra Nevada Mountains
(D) American Mountains

(14) What is the longest mountain range in North America?
(A) Rocky Mountains
(B) Appalachian Mountains
(C) Sierra Nevada Mountains
(D) Mountains of the Moon

(15) What is the longest river in the United States?
(A) The Missouri River
(B) The Mississippi River
(C) The Mander River
(D) The Rocky River

(16) Today, we can use GPS and maps on our cell phones.
   (A) True
   (B) False

(17) The Appalachian Mountains run from Canada to New Mexico.
   (A) True
   (B) False

(18) The Chihuahuan Desert exists mainly between Montana and Northern California.
   (A) True
   (B) False

(19) California is in the "West" region of the United States.
   (A) True
   (B) False

(20) A political map is used to identify features such as mountains, rivers, and deserts.
   (A) True
   (B) False

Quiz Answers

1. **B.** "Geography" translates to "earth description."
2. **C.** "Scale" helps readers measure distances.
3. **B.** "Key" helps readers identify markers on a map.
4. **D.** The compass helps readers identify directions.
5. **B.** A physical map displays mountains, rivers, deserts, and physical features.
6. **A.** A political map displays city names, country borders, and cultural features.
7. **B.** "H.O.M.E.S." helps you remember the initials for the Great Lakes.
8. **D.** The South American Ocean is not a major ocean.
9. **D.** The Midsouth is not an official region of the United States.
10. **A.** A rural area is composed of mostly farmland, without many houses or communities.
11. **C.** An area that is composed of mostly tall buildings and apartments and is tight on space is an urban area.
12. **B.** An area with a steady population and a mix of community and business is a suburban area.
13. **B.** In early American history, the Appalachian Mountains served as a border between the east coast and the west.
14. **A.** The Rocky Mountains are the longest mountain range in North America.
15. **A.** The Missouri River is the longest river in the United States.
16. **True.** Today, we can use GPS and maps on our cell phones.
17. **False.** The Appalachian Mountains run from Maine to Alabama.
18. **False.** The Chihuahuan Desert exists in Mexico and the southwest United States.
19. **True.** California is in the "West" region of the United States.
20. **False.** A political map is used to identify city names, country borders, and cultural features.

Section 3: Government and Law

Each person needs to live according to a set of rules; our government, the organization that leads our country is essential is creating these rules. But they cannot do it alone. Much of the time, they turn to the people to see what the people want. Discussions are held, votes are cast, and though it can be slow, the system will change. Here, we will explore how laws work, how the government works, and how they are connected. We will end with discussing how our government interacts with the leadership from other countries, and how this all affects our every day life; essentially, why should any of this matter to you? What part can you play in your country?

If you want to understand law in America, the first you will want to know is the United States Constitution. Some background on the Constitution: in the late 1700s, the thirteen original American colonies were in rebellion against their mother country, Great Britain. After the colonists had defeated the British, they needed to create their new American government. They realized that they should begin with a basic set of rules, and they penned a document that proclaimed themselves to be a country. This document is known as the *United States Constitution.*

Creating the Constitution was not a simple task; it was worked on by men across the colonies, each of which had his own idea about how the government should be run. After the first draft of the Constitution was issued, ten *amendments* (changes) were made to it. These ten amendments became known as the Bill of Rights, and are as follows:

Amendment I - Congress shall make no law respecting an establishment of religion, or prohibiting the free exercise thereof; or abridging the freedom of speech, or of the press; or the right of the people peaceably to assemble, and to petition the government for a redress of grievances.

Amendment II - A well regulated militia, being necessary to the security of a free state, the right of the people to keep and bear arms, shall not be infringed.

Amendment II - No soldier shall, in time of peace be quartered in any house, without the consent of the owner, nor in time of war, but in a manner to be prescribed by law.

Amendment IV - The right of the people to be secure in their persons, houses, papers, and effects, against unreasonable searches and seizures, shall not be violated, and no warrants shall issue, but upon probable cause, supported by oath or affirmation, and particularly describing the place to be searched, and the persons or things to be seized.

Amendment V - No person shall be held to answer for a capital, or otherwise infamous crime, unless on a presentment or indictment of a grand jury, except in cases arising in the land or naval forces, or in the militia, when in actual service in time of war or public danger; nor shall any person be subject for the same offense to be twice put in jeopardy of life or limb; nor shall be compelled in any criminal case to be a witness against himself, nor be deprived of life, liberty, or property, without due process of law; nor shall private property be taken for public use, without just compensation.

Amendment VI - In all criminal prosecutions, the accused shall enjoy the right to a speedy and public trial, by an impartial jury of the state and district wherein the crime shall have been committed, which district shall have been previously ascertained by law, and to be informed of the nature and cause of the accusation; to be confronted with the witnesses against him; to have compulsory process for obtaining witnesses in his favor, and to have the assistance of counsel for his defense.

Amendment VII - In suits at common law, where the value in controversy shall exceed twenty dollars, the right of trial by jury shall be preserved, and no fact tried by a jury, shall be otherwise reexamined in any court of the United States, than according to the rules of the common law.

Amendment VIII - Excessive bail shall not be required, nor excessive fines imposed, nor cruel and unusual punishments inflicted.

Amendment IX - The enumeration in the Constitution, of certain rights, shall not be construed to deny or disparage others retained by the people.

Amendment X - The powers not delegated to the United States by the Constitution, nor prohibited by it to the states, are reserved to the states respectively, or to the people.

Currently, there are twenty-seven amendments to the Constitution, and each one must be agreed upon by both branches of *Congress*, part of our government. Congress is made up of two parts: the Senate, and the House of Representatives.

The House of Representatives is a group of people that come from each of the United States. The bigger the population in the state, the more representatives you have. For example, North Dakota, South Dakota, Vermont, Wyoming, Delaware, and Alaska all have very small populations, so they each get one representative. On the other end of the stick, California has the largest state population and has fifty-three representatives. Each representative stands for a certain of people in that state, and they vote based on what the people want. They work with laws and try to pass them. The House of Representatives is responsible for creating bills that will require the United States to spend money; for that reason, the House is a very important part of our government! The people vote for new representatives every two years.

The Senate is made up of exactly two people from each state, no matter what the population is. They work with other countries and have the power to accept or reject treaties (offers of peace). In order to be a senator, you need to have been a United States citizen for nine years, be at least thirty years old, and live in the state that you want to represent in the Senate. It is a tough job, but someone has to do it!

Now we will discuss how laws are created, and we are going to use the example: in 2013, a member of the House of Representatives introduced a bill called the *Family Engagement in Education Act*, which wanted to give assistance to families that wanted to be more involved in their children's education and help them with their schooling.

When the bill was introduced, a small committee was tasked with looking over the bill, finding faults with it, approving it, and so on. Right now, it is still in review. If the committee decides that the bill is not a good idea, they will set it aside and focus on more important issues. If they decide that it is a good idea, they will present the bill to the House of Representatives, where a vote is held.

If the House of Representatives passes the bill, it is then sent to the Senate. A committee consisting of members of both the Senate and the House review the bill and again try to find any faults with it. Once they have worked out all the kinks, the bill is presented to the Senate and another vote is held. The Speaker of the House and the Vice President will sign the bill, and then it is sent to the President of the United States, awaiting his signature.

It may seem like this is a simple job that flows quite easily, but in reality Congress faces thousands of bills each year, about six thousand. Imagine how much reading, reviewing, and discussing you have to do as a Congressman or Congresswoman!

There can often be complications with finalizing the law, however. For example, it can take months or years for a bill to pass through the House of Representatives and Congress, arrive at the President's desk, and the President refuses to sign it. In this case, the bill then returns to Congress for reevaluation. If two-thirds of Congress still decides to uphold the bill, then it will be passed even without the President's consent. If the two-thirds is not met, then the bill dies and is tucked away.

Sometimes, the people believe that a law is unjust or broken. They call and email their state representatives and senators and create a movement that petitions for change. The congressmen will then bring it to the attention of their respective houses of congress and analyze the law. Again, it may take a long time; some congressmen are sure to believe that the law does not need to be changed, while others are sure that it does. After a tug-and-war battle of opinions, the bill will either remain unchanged or become something better or worse, depending on what our congress decides.

All of this is referred to as the *legislative branch* of the government. They work on creating and carrying out laws, and they work tightly with the other two branches of government: *executive* (the president and his cabinet) and *judicial* (the Supreme Court and the court systems).

While the majority of people follow the law, there are people that break it. In the case that the rules are broken, we need to have a system for punishing and correcting the wrongdoer. This is where another branch of the government comes in: the Judicial Branch. The judicial system of the United States is led by the Supreme Court, which was created in the Constitution. The Supreme Court is the highest judicial power in the country; there are currently nine justices (judges) that sit on the court, and throughout the year, they take cases that are of the highest importance to the country. Recently, they have been looking into the issue of gay rights in America, and whether states are allowed to ban gay marriage, or should allow everyone to be married.

Below the Supreme Court are federal courts (run by the government), state courts (belonging to each individual state), and city courts (belonging to each individual city). When a person has committed a crime or broken a law, they will go to one of these courts. Small crimes (like stealing) will likely lead to sessions at town or city courts, while larger crimes (like trying to hurt someone else) will likely take place on the state level.

For an example, let us say that a man gets sent to prison for stealing a DVD from a convenience store. The storeowner catches the man stealing and calls the police; law enforcement finds the man and arrests him. When someone is arrested, they are read their "Miranda rights," which follow this statement:

"You have the right to remain silent. Anything you say can and will be held against you in the court of law. You have the right to an attorney. If you cannot afford an attorney, one will be provided for you."

A police officer is required to read this to everyone he or she arrests; it essentially means that the criminal does not have to speak if they do not want to (because the Fifth Amendment declares that the person only needs to speak in court). However, anything that the criminal says could be used as evidence against him in court (like if the criminal denied committing the crime, or something like that). The criminal is entitled to have a lawyer defend them in court, and if they are too poor to pay a lawyer, the government will give them one. If you have ever watched a show that involves law enforcement officers, you have probably heard them shout the famous Miranda rights at some point.

From there, the court case will begin. Once the defendant (the criminal, who is defending himself from the government's accusations) has a lawyer, a *jury* is selected. A jury is a group of random citizens that are selected to listen in on the court case and make a ruling. The jury will consist of people from across the community, of different ages, races, and genders. Before the civil rights movement in the 1960s, it was common for African-American defendants to be met with an all-white, racist jury who would hopelessly condemn innocent defendants. Today, however, juries are much diverse to account for a variety of backgrounds and opinions.

It is the judge's duty to oversee the case and make sure everything goes correctly and smoothly. A judge will only ever decide a case if both the government and defendant ask for it. Most of the time, however, it is a jury that makes the final call. It is the judge, though, that decides the punishment. Lesser crimes will receive smaller sentences, and for more dangerous crimes the convicted criminal could be put away for months, years, or in the worst case, for life. Sometimes, along with a jail sentence, the criminal is also forced to pay a certain sum of money.

Many people do not know that there is a difference between "jail" and "prison." When a person is sent to "jail," it is often a smaller county facility, and for less than a year. Someone who commits a felony, or a very serious crime, will go to "prison" for over a year. Felonies are also punishable by death, depending on how severe it is. Felonies are taken care of by state or federal courts. Being sent to jail or prison is officially known as *incarceration*, a crucial word to know if you want to understand how our law system works.

Next, we will move to how the United States interacts with other countries. To start off, the first person you will want to know is the *Secretary of State*, who is the person who talks with other countries' leaders and politicians, sometimes to ease tension in times of stress or war. As of this writing, the United States Secretary of State is politician John Kerry; before him was Hillary Clinton, who allegedly has plans to run in the 2016 presidential election, and who is married to the 42nd President of the United States, Bill Clinton. In addition to the national Secretary of State, however, each state has their own that works in conjunction with each other.

While it not the Secretary of State's job to regulate trade between countries, it does play a large part in his or her every day life. Trade is essential for all countries; we trade to get things that we do not have much of here. There are two words you will want to understand to learn about trade:

Import: An import is something that *comes into the* country. For example, you would say that the United States receives imports of clothes, oil, and other goods from around the world.

Export: An export is something that *leaves the* country. For example, you would say that the top United States exports are machinery and electronics, as of 2013.

Trade is great for the American economy. While we spend money bringing goods into the country, we also receive billions of dollars selling our materials to other country. It gets our economy going and makes our stores vibrant and full of goods. Next time you wear a shirt, check the tag and see what country it was made in! You might be surprised where all your stuff comes from!

Now that you know how the United States interacts with other countries on a financial level, let us discuss peace and war. Throughout its relatively short history, the United States has been at military odds with many other countries: Britain, Mexico, Spain, Germany, Japan, North Vietnam, and others. The Constitution instructs us on how our government makes treaties with other countries. A *treaty* is a symbol of alliance between two countries; sometimes it is just a gesture of friendship, while other times it is an agreement to stop fighting. There are a few steps in creating a treaty and making sure it goes through.

In the first step, American representatives, such as the Secretary of State, will engage in conversation and discussion with the opposing country and try to reach an agreement. This may take a while, to accommodate everyone's wishes. Sometimes, sacrifices must be made in the name of peace. Once this has been approved by all of the representatives, it is then sent to the United States president (and likewise the leaders of the other country).

The President of the United States now has a choice to make: to sign the treaty, or not to sign the treaty? If he believes that the treaty is absolutely for the good of the American people, he will sign it. If not, the representatives must start over again and broker an agreement that the president will approve. In the case that the president thinks the treaty is a good idea, he signs it and then it is distributed to members of the Senate in Congress for approval.

The Senate, like we discussed earlier, is now in charge of approving or rejecting the treaty. *Two-thirds* of the Senate must approve. But why two-thirds? Why is this number so important? The United States is made of two political parties: *Republicans* and *Democrats*. The government does not want Congress to be split exactly 50-50, so they require that more than half of the Senate approve the treaty. That way, Republicans do not just vote for Republican views, and Democrats do not just vote for Democrat views. It forces people to make sacrifices and look out for the interest of the country.

By now, you should have a basic understanding of how laws work in the United States. From their conception to being carried out, to being broken and to being fixed, laws are a complicated but necessary part of American society. International relations, also, affect us every single day and are crucial if we want to understand the country around us. The discussion and activities section will hopefully widen your comprehension and force you to apply your knowledge. One day, you will become an active member of American society, and it begins here with your education!

Discussion Questions

(1) As you go about your daily life, do the rules set by the Constitution have any effect on you? Which ones? Why are they important?

(2) Why is a Constitution important, especially for a country that has just been formed? What would happen if a country did not have a proper Constitution, or document that sets down rules?

(3) Which one is more important: the House of Representatives or the Senate? Or do they balance each other out?

(4) When it comes to the process of a law being created, do you think there are any improvements that we can make? Do you think it is a system that flows smoothly? What changes would you make if you could?

(5) If you had the chance to introduce one bill into Congress, which bill would you choose and why? Discuss why this subject is important to you. Keep this in mind for the Activities section.

(6) Do you think it's a good idea to have a Supreme Court? What is good about having nine judges that rule over all the courts? Is there anything bad about this? Would you change anything if you could?

(7) Why are Miranda rights important to someone who has been arrested? What might happen if the police officer does not read them?

(8) What is the difference between jail and prison? What sorts of crimes accompany both of these locations?

(9) What is a treaty, and why is it important to the American country and its people? What advantages does it have? Are there any disadvantages?

(10) What is the difference between an import and an export? Why is it important that we buy from other countries, and that we sell to them too?

Activities

(1) Paraphrase each article of the Bill of Rights; after you've done so, write one or two sentences about each article and explain why it is important.

(2) Layer two pieces of paper on top of each; fold them in half. You now have a small "book." Now, choose either the House of Representatives or the Senate and do a research project on them. Draw a cover, and then on the inside of the book, talk about who is in that house of congress, what they do, why they're important, how they get elected, and so on. Feel free to get creative and colorful!

(3) For whatever house you *did not* choose for Activity 2, pretend you are now a member of that house. Imagine what your normal day is like, and write a short journal entry from the perspective of a Congressman. Have fun with this activity, and feel free to do any additional research.

(4) Watch the following video, "I'm Just A Bill" from Schoolhouse Rock. Afterwards, create a timeline of each step the bill goes through, using arrows to indicate where it goes between each step. https://www.youtube.com/watch?v=FFroMQlKiag

(5) Remember Discussion Question 5? Pretend that you are a Congressman and you are going to introduce a bill. Choose a house of Congress to be in, and then decide what you want to change about the country (it can be something serious like raising teachers' salaries, or something funny like making pizza a mandatory breakfast meal). Write journal entries about how the bill does in Congress, and how the people react. Do other Congressmen not like your bill? How does the public think? Does it pass the House? The Senate? Does the President sign it?

(6) Watch the following video about the three branches of government. Afterwards, create three columns on a piece of paper. Each column will be a different branch of government. Write about what each branch does and why it is important to the United States. https://www.youtube.com/watch?v=x5M50xBz1cU

(7) On your own, complete some research about the Supreme Court and answer the following questions on a separate piece of paper: How many justices are on the Supreme Court? Were there always nine justices? Who selects the justices? How much power do they have? What are famous cases they have received in previous years? Afterwards, watch this entertaining clip from *Sesame Street*, featuring Supreme Court Justice Sonia Sotomayor. https://www.youtube.com/watch?v=FizspmIJbAw

(8) Imagine that you are a police officer and that you have just arrested someone for a crime (of your choosing). Write about what happens to them as they go through the justice system; how are they punished? Who decides the punishment? Is there a jury? What does the jury decide? Feel free to make this exciting and suspenseful!

(9) On a piece of paper, write out the differences between an "import" and an "export." Then, doing some research online or in the library, find some of the United States' most popular imports and exports. After that, research the most popular ones for your own state!

(10) Now that you have studied government and law, watch this final video on the Constitution. Stop the video at 10:45, unless you want to participate in the quiz section after the video. When you have finished, write down five important things that you have learned in this section; in addition, write down any questions that you might have, and try to use research to find the answers!
https://www.youtube.com/watch?v=WEy4sg2-kp4

For Further Reading

Barnes, Peter W. *Cappy Tail's Capitol Tale.* VSP Books, 2010.

Barnes, Peter W. *House Mouse, Senate Mouse.* Little Patriot Press, 2012.

Barnes, Peter W. *Marshall, the Courthouse Mouse: A Tail of the U.S. Supreme Court.* Little Patriot Press, 2012.

Dubois, Muriel L. *The U.S. Supreme Court.* Capstone Press, 2000.

Firestone, Mary. *The State Judicial Branch.* Capstone Press, 2000.

Firestone, Mary. *The State Legislative Branch.* Capstone Press, 2000.

Higgins, Nadia. *US Government Through Infographics.* Lerner Publishing Group, 2014.

J.D., Syl Sobel. *The U.S. Constitution and You.* Barron's Educational Series, 2012.

Kennedy, Edward. *My Senator and Me: A Dog's Eye View of Washington, D.C.* Scholastic, Inc., 2006.

Lane, Brian and Laura Buller. *Crime and Detection.* DK Publishing, 2005.

Reis, Ronald A. *The US Congress for Kids: Over 20 Years of Lawmaking, Deal-Breaking, and Compromising, with 21 Activities.* Chicago Review Press, 2014.

See, Betty. *Jury Trials in the Classroom.* Prufrock press, 2005.

See, Betty. *More Jury Trials in the Classroom.* Prufrock Press, 2007.

Trounstine, Connie Remlinger. *Fingerprints on the Table: The Story of the White House Treaty Table.* White House Historical Association, 2013.

Van Wie, Nancy. *Travels with Max to the Supreme Court.* Max's Publications, 1994.

Quiz

(1) What document sets down the rules for our country, and contains amendments decided upon by Congress?
   (A) The Declaration of Independence
   (B) The Bill of Rights
   (C) The Constitution
   (D) The Federalist Papers

(2) The first ten amendments are called the _____.
   (A) Constitution
   (B) Bill of Rights
   (C) Federalist
   (D) Miranda rights

(3) Congress is made up of the _____ and the _____.
   (A) Senate; Constitution
   (B) Senate; House of Representatives
   (C) House of Representatives; Miranda rights
   (D) Constitution; Senate of Representatives

(4) Which house of Congress is allowed to create bills that spend money?
   (A) The Senate
   (B) The House of Representatives
   (C) Both of them are allowed to create bills that spend money
   (D) Neither of them; that is a decision for the President and Secretary of State

(5) Which house of Congress is allowed to approve treaties?
   (A) The Senate
   (B) The House of Representatives
   (C) Both of them must approve treaties; if not, it gets sent back to the President
   (D) Neither of them; only the President can approve a treaty

(6) If a president refuses to sign a bill passed by Congress, can the bill still be passed?
   (A) No; if the President does not sign the bill, it is discarded.
   (B) Yes; if the President does not sign the bill, it is passed anyways.
   (C) Yes; if the President does not sign the bill, it returns to Congress, who can overrule the President.
   (D) Yes; if the President does not sign the bill, it sits in a desk until a new president takes office, and that president is forced to sign it.

(7) Congress is part of the _____ branch of the United States government.
   (A) Executive
   (B) Judicial
   (C) Legislative
   (D) Constitutional

(8) The judicial system is led by nine justices who sit on the _____.

(A) Constitutional Committee
(B) Secretary of State's court
(C) Supreme Court
(D) Judicial Courthouse

(9) When a person is arrested, a police officer must read him/her the _____.
    (A) Miranda rights
    (B) Article IV of the Constitution
    (C) Bill of Rights
    (D) Preamble rights

(10) What is a jury?
    (A) A group of judges that work together to decide the fate of a criminal
    (B) A group of randomly selected citizens that decide if a criminal is guilty or innocent
    (C) A group of randomly selected citizens that decide a criminal's punishment
    (D) A group of criminals that decide the fate of another criminal in court

(11) What is the duty of the Secretary of State?
    (A) To work with other countries and foreign affairs
    (B) To monitor how the President is doing his job
    (C) To spy on other countries and detect potential threats
    (D) To tour the country and make sure that each state governor is working well with their fellow politicians

(12) What is a treaty?
    (A) An alliance between two or more countries
    (B) A declaration of war against another nation
    (C) An agreement to temporarily postpone war until another time
    (D) A document that discusses the details of trade between two countries

(13) If the President of the United States approves a treaty, what is the next step?
    (A) It is immediately put into action
    (B) The American people vote on whether to accept it
    (C) It goes to the leader of the other country; if he or she says yes, it is immediately accepted
    (D) It goes to Congress to be decided upon

(14) When Congress votes upon a treaty, what percentage of them *must* approve in order for the treaty to be accepted?
    (A) One-half
    (B) One-third
    (C) Two-thirds
    (D) All of them

(15) An _____ is something that we purchase from another country and have it sent to us.
    (A) Treaty
    (B) Miranda
    (C) Export
    (D) Import

(16) An export is something that the United States sells and ships to other countries.
   (A) True
   (B) False

(17) A judge is *always* the one that decides if a criminal is innocent or guilty.
   (A) True
   (B) False

(18) It is the duty of a jury to decide the punishment of a criminal.
   (A) True
   (B) False

(19) There are ten amendments in the Bill of Rights.
   (A) True
   (B) False

(20) The Constitution was created when America broke off from the British Empire.
   (A) True
   (B) False

Quiz Answers

(1) **C.** The Constitution sets down the rules for our country, and contains amendments decided upon by Congress.

(2) **B.** The first ten amendments are called the Bill of Rights.

(3) **B.** The Senate is made up of the Senate and the House of Representatives.

(4) **B.** The House of Representatives is allowed to approve treaties.

(5) **A.** The Senate is allowed to approve treaties.

(6) **C.** If the President refuses to sign a bill, it returns to Congress, who can overrule the President.

(7) **C.** Congress is part of the legislative branch of the United States government.

(8) **C.** The judicial system is led by nine justices who sit on the Supreme Court.

(9) **A.** When a person is arrested, a police officer must read him/her the Miranda rights.

(10) **B.** A jury is a group of randomly selected citizens that decide if a criminal is guilty or innocent.

(11) **A.** The Secretary of State works with other countries and foreign affairs.

(12) **A.** A treaty is an alliance between two or more countries.

(13) **D.** If a president approves a treaty, it goes to Congress to be decided upon.

(14) **C.** When Congress votes upon a treaty, two-thirds of them must approve it.

(15) **D.** An import is something that we purchase from another country and have it send

(16) **True.** An export is something that the United States sells and ships to other countries.

(17) **False.** A judge is not always the one who decides if someone is innocent or guilty; most often that is the decision of a jury.

(18) **False.** A jury does not decide on a punishment; that is the duty of a judge.

(19) **True.** There are ten amendments in the Bill of Rights.

(20) **True.** The Constitution was created when America broke off from the British Empire.

Section 4: Economics

In the previous section, we very briefly discussed trade. You learned key words such as *import* and *export* and how countries interacted with each other, especially when it came to trade and finances. Now, we are going to delve further into the subject of *economics*.

Economics is anything to do with, basically, money. It deals with how we produce money, how we spend it, and how we share it. At a single point, there is a set point of money in the world, and it is constantly being spent. To use a simple example, let us say that you buy a two dollar candy bar on the way to your friend's house. That two dollars goes to the store, and the store needs money to (1) pay its employees (2) pay for the building itself (3) buy more candy, along with other minute expenses. The two dollars you just spent may go into the hands of one of the workers, who may use it for anything. Many *economists* are concerned with how money flows from one hand to another. The field of economy is a vast and complicated field.

To help you understand, we are going to begin at the most basic level: *Want* and *Need*. These two words describe everything that we ever buy in life: we either *want* it, or we *need* it. We *need* food to survive, but within the subject of "food," there are wants and needs. You need vitamins and important nutrients to survive; these are needs. You want candy, for example, but it's not necessary. You need a house; you want a mansion. Do you see how that works? You *need* water, you *want* soda. Next time you're spending money at the store, think about these two subjects.

So why is this important? Why should you know about Want and Need? Well, it all depends on how much money you have. If you are a little tight for money and you need to save up, you will focus your spending only on the needs. But, if you have extra, you can focus on your spending on both Wants and Needs. More spending by you means that more people are getting money (you buying a candy bar may lead to someone getting money in a paycheck). People like it when they have money to spend on wants; it means you are in a good place.

Now that that's out of the way, we are going to move to another simple subject: *Supply* and *Demand*. To explain this, we are going to imagine that you are the owner of a small fruit store. You are independently owned; you are not part of a larger company.

Your *supply* is what you have in store. Each day, you might count your supply of fruit: apples, bananas, strawberries, and so on. *Demand* is what people want. Let's say that there was a fruit store across from you, and customers either went to your store or the other fruit store. Your demand might not be so high, because customers are going to your rival store. For example, let's say that you sell 100 piece of fruit per day. But suddenly, the other store closes down. Now, all of the customers are going to go to *your* store. The *demand* is suddenly going to rise, because you have more customers that want more fruit.

If your demand goes up, can you keep the same amount of *supply*? No way! If you sold 100 pieces of fruit per day before, you will have to raise your supply. That means that you will have to put in the money to buy more fruit.

Supply and *Demand* also affects the price of an object. Let's say that, before your rise in demand, you paid 25 cents for each apple and then sold that apple for one dollar. Now that the demand has increased, you might increase your prices (because now customers are forced to go to your store, so you are more likely to get willing customers to pay whatever to get fruit!). So let's say that you now raise your prices to $2 for each apple, because the customers have nowhere else to get their fruit.

Have you ever really wanted a popular phone? Like an iPhone? Or an iPod? They are so expensive because they are in such high demand; people love using them, so Apple (the company that makes them) knows that they can charge higher prices and people will still pay for them.

Just as prices will rise if demand rises, so too do prices drop if demand drops. Let's say that apples suddenly went out of style and people didn't want to eat them anymore. Then, people *certainly* would not pay $2 for an apple. In order to attract people to buy your apples, you would need to lower your price.

This is not *always* true, however. A couple years ago, there was a sudden shortage of chicken wings. The *supply* went down, but the *demand* was still high. People wanted chicken wings still, so companies had to raise the prices so they still received enough money for fewer products. Consumers were upset about rising prices.

So why is this important? Why is this at the heart of economics? Well, when you run a store, you need to *purchase your supply* ahead of time. Let's say each week that you buy two thousand apples, and on average sell two thousand per week. You sell the apples for more than you buy them, so that you can make money. But if people stop buying apples, you suddenly have too many apples and no one to buy them—so you lower your price. But now you are *losing money* because you are selling them for less than you *normally do*. Hopefully, this all makes sense! There will be more on this in the Discussion and Activities section.

Essentially, everyone in our society needs to worry about supply and demand, just as they need to worry about Want and Need. On the same page, everyone is a buyer—we purchase houses, cars, food, and clothes. A few select people are sellers, the ones who own companies or work in stores and try to earn money by (1) knowing what people want to buy (2) attracting them to buy it. Sellers need to know how to get their customers to buy their product.

There are two different types of sale: goods and service. *Good* is a term commonly used to describe an object that is sold, like clothes or food. Goods are imported and exported, based on *demand*. If the United States population continues to grow, then the demand for clothes will go up, which means we will import more clothes (goods) from other countries. On the other side of the coin, *service* is something like education (teachers), hair cuts (barbers), paint your nails (salon), and other jobs like that. These places do not offer you goods that you can take home, but their objective is to serve you in some way that costs money.

One final key term you will want to know is *interdependence*, which is very different from the word *independence*. *Independence* means that you are strong enough to be yourself and do not need to rely on anyone else for support; *interdependence* is the exact opposite, meaning that you rely on others for some of your *needs*. You can probably assume that you are interdependent, unless you live out in the words with barely any interaction. You rely on others for your clothes, your house, and your car, almost all of your material possessions. Farmers produce most of their own food, but they still may visit the store; and unless they built all of their machinery by themselves, they most likely purchased it.

As mentioned before, a good can be a food. But before the food reaches you, it must go through a production process of its own. Fruits and vegetables are often picked from a tree/the ground/a bush, cleaned, and then shipped to a store. But other foods, such as chips, meat, bread, and more must go through a production process before you get them.

For example, bread is made from wheat, flower, and yeast. It doesn't just pop out of the ground in a loaf, bagged, and then sent to a store. Bread starts as a dough made of both flour and wheat, that is then mixed with yeast, something that helps it rise when it bakes in the oven. Centuries ago, people used to make their own bread instead of buying it at the store; it was cheaper that way! But now it is easier to produce millions of loaves of bread and ship them out, receiving money back.

Anything that is not entirely fresh is considered processed food – including milk! Today, the milk is taken from the cow and then pasteurized (any diseases or bugs inside are killed), which makes it safe for us to drink. The milk is then turned into different kinds: skim, 1%, 2%, or whole milk (skim milk is relatively fat-free and has little cream in it, while whole milk has much more fat and cream). Milk can also be turned into other dairy products, such as cheese, yogurt, butter, or cream.

As mentioned in the previous paragraph, all milk is pasteurized. This word was named after a man named Louis Pasteur, who a French scientist who studied the human body and diseases. Before he came along, milk often made people sick. When it comes directly from the cow, it is not safe to drink. It has germs and microorganisms inside it that can lead to disease. Louis Pasteur set out on a way in which people could drink milk, not get sick, and still get the same good flavor.

This occurred in the middle of the 1800s, when many scientists were just learning about germs and disease. They had not yet realized that germs (bacteria and other dangerous microorganisms) caused people to be sick. But Pasteur followed this idea, and it changed how we handled dairy products forever. Now, all of your milk is processed and pasteurized so that it is safe to drink.

That's just one way that your food is processed. People also use the weather and water to actively grow and process their food, especially farmers. Using water to help your farmland and crops is a process called *irrigation*, and it is widespread across the world. All farmers, if they hope to be successful, must choose areas that will receive enough rain each year, which is why you do not see many farms in hot, desert places. If you *do* choose a hotter area, you may have to water your crops yourself, instead of letting the weather do it for you.

Also in these areas, farmers will build *irrigation systems* to get water to their crops. In ancient times, the easiest way to irrigate your crops was simply to fill buckets with water and bring it to your crops; but as people, technology, and society evolved, new methods were created.

Many farmers created (and still do today) *irrigation canals,* small waterways that carry water from a main source (ocean, river, stream, etc.) towards the farmland. So that the water was never absorbed by soil, farmers usually lined the canals with stone. Instead of carrying water in buckets from rivers, the water would flow from the rivers towards the farmland, majorly depleting the workload for farmers.

Irrigation canals made it a lot simpler to grow more crops such as *wheat,* one of the key components of bread. It has been around for thousands upon thousands of years, and has been eaten by humans for at least seventy thousand years. Eventually, as humans transitioned from a society of nomadic hunters to a society of settling farmers, we stopped just picking wheat up and eating it, and started cultivating it—farming it, growing it, and so on. Around ten thousand years ago, humans discovered that you could cook wheat, and even make it into bread!

Here, we will discuss how you begin with thin wheat straws and end up with a loaf of bread in your kitchen! Note that this process evolved over thousands of years, and was especially improved with the design and creation of mills.

It begins in a small building called the silo, in which the wheat is cleaned (you never know what could be on it from the fields, like bugs) and then it is dried. In the next building, the screen room, a machine called "the separator" makes sure only the wheat is being processed, and not any excess scraps of straw or grass. After that, it is moved into the official "Mill" building (you may recognize it from its four-pronged fan).

There are four steps in the mill.

(1) The wheat seeds are run through rolls that crack the seeds open. The inside of the seeds are called *semolina,* and the outer shell is called *starch* and *bran.* Next, the grain rockets up to the top floor of the mill.
(2) On the top floor, a gizmo called the "Plansifter" takes out the bran and starch. The Plansifter contains numerous *sieves,* kind of like strainers, that filter out everything but the pure wheat. On the sieves floor, many farmers also add vitamins to the wheat to give it nutritional value.
(3) Once the wheat is sifted through the sieves, it drops down to a floor known as the Purifier. This floor makes sure that all the wheat is of the same texture to make sure the bread is as smooth and pure as possible. Any piece that is too big is sent back up to the top floor (the sieves) to be sifted through again.
(4) On the final floor, the wheat is rolled down into flour. Essentially, the whole purpose of the mill is to grind wheat seeds down into flour powder. That is it for the mill; the flour will then turn into bread once it arrives in a baker's hands.

It is the baker's job to take the flour and make loaves of bread. The baker has an enormous mixing bowl, where the flour is joined with water, fat, salt, and especially *yeast.* Yeast is a type of fungus that will eventually give off gas that helps the bread rise—expand upwards into a loaf of bread! It will take about twenty minutes to stir all of these ingredients neatly together.

Bakers will then take this mixture and turn it into different shapes: flat loaf-shapes for loaves of bread, balls to make buns (hamburger, hot dog, and so on), longer pieces for baguettes, and so on. Imagine all the different shapes of bread there are! They are then sent into an area called a Proover, in which the yeast goes to work. All the bread shapes then lift up and take their normal shapes. It is then sent into an enormous oven, where it takes a half hour to bake. After being cooled, it is then okay to dispatch to bakeries and stores across the world.

This is not a new way of producing bread; it has been around for a few hundred years; as our population grows, people keep on finding new and innovative ways to increase our production of bread so that everyone might have enough. Just think of how much wheat you consume: bread, bagels, pizza, bread crumbs, cereal, potato chips, and more. Wheat is an important part of our society, and the production behind it is a fascinating subject. The more you know about production, the more you know about how our economy works.

We will now turn our glance to the effect of supply on production. Once again, we will use the example of chicken wings. A few years ago, many people noted the rising price of chicken wings and, in fact, chicken in general. They wondered what the reason was—and many companies pointed to the insane popularity of chicken wings. Chicken wings are often seen as a food to eat during parties and while watching sports, and as sports become more popular, people get together more to watch sports. This increases the *demand* for chicken wings, even though the *supply* is low.

Tom Super, a member of the National Chicken Council, claimed that "Birds only have two wings, so there is already a somewhat limited suppl. It is not economically feasible for companies to raise birds just for the wings."

We use all parts of the chicken: the breasts, the tenders, the wings, and the wings are in higher demand than the rest of the chicken, leading to a problem in the supply area, which then leads to a problem in the production area, which then leads to frustration in the demand area. This demonstrates that if the resources are low, everything else will be thrown into tension.

Hopefully this has cast some light on the subject of economics and production. The main objective here is to see the relationship between the two: the production of food is directly related to supply and demand, which affects the money in our pockets. There were a number of key concepts here that will be useful to know in the future, and even more important to study the links between them:

Import & Export

Want & Need

Supply & Demand

Buyer & Seller

Interdependence & Independence

Production and economy is constantly flowing cycle; supply and demand is constantly shifting, and the weather is even a big factor. Chicken wings are more popular from January to March because of sports season; bacon is more popular in the summer; you are much more likely to see peppermint flavors in the winter, pumpkin flavors in the autumn. Demand for pumpkins are higher in the autumn than in the spring, so farmers and sellers must plan accordingly.

Once you understand the tenuous relationships between these subjects, you will have a basic understanding of our economy and why it is so complicated to operate. Hopefully this has acted as a simple overview!

Discussion Questions

(1) Briefly discuss the relationship between *supply* and *demand*. Does one go up when one goes down? Try to come up with some possibilities.

(2) You learned about import and export in the last section—imagine ways in which imports and exports might affect supply and demand, or the other way around. Consider how the weather affects farmers!

(3) Think about some things in your life that you want, versus what you need. In your room and your house, what do you have that is a *need*? What do you have that is a *want*? Keep this in mind for the Activities section.

(4) What is the difference between *goods* and *service*? In your life, what do you have that is a good? Have you ever paid for a *service*?

(5) Explain the difference between *independence* and *interdependence*. How are they different in terms of the United States economy?

(6) Why is it important that we pasteurize milk? Should all foods be processed and checked for disease? What do you think?

(7) What is irrigation, and why is it important to farmers? Does it make life easier or harder, and why?

(8) Are you surprised that there are so many steps to producing bread? Did you think it was a lot simpler? Will that change your view on how you look at bread in the store now?

(9) Chicken wings were used as a common example to demonstrate supply and demand. Discuss the chicken wing problem, and why it had an effect on the economy. Essentially, why did prices go up? Make sure to talk about supply and demand.

(10) Do you have a better understanding of *economy*, now that you know about supply and demand, want and need, and buyer and seller? Briefly talk about how these three concepts work together to form the basic groundwork for our money system. How is money involved in all of this?

Activities

(1) On a piece of paper, create two columns. One will be "Want" and one will be "Need." List ten objects each that you want, and then that you need. Ask your parent or guardian for help; but only if you *need* it, not want it!

(2) We are going to return to the hypothetical situation in which you are running a fruit store/fruit stand. Write a series of journal entries, and be sure to include information about supply and demand. How is business from day to day? Is there any competition in the area, any other stores? Does demand go up? Go down? How do you change your supply? Write at least three journal entries, and feel free to get really creative!

(3) The invention of money was something that was not really discussed, but was an important development for trade. Watch the following Schoolhouse Rock video, and afterwards write a quick paragraph about how *money* (coins, paper money, etc.) affected how people sold and bought goods. https://www.youtube.com/watch?v=wHY5cdExNa8

(4) Create two more columns on a piece of paper. One column will be "Independence," and the other will be "Interdependence." List anything that you are interdependent on (what do you buy?), and anything for which you are independent (do you make anything completely by yourself; it's okay if you don't!).

(5) Watch the following video about Herschel's World of Economics: Good and Services, which offers a humorous lesson about the difference between goods and services. At the end, list anything that you might have learned in the video that you did not know before. https://www.youtube.com/watch?v=wy0TrDCiqLw

(6) Do some outside research on Louis Pasteur. Create a short biography for him on paper (and include drawings if you want!). Be sure to include the creation of pasteurization, and define what germ theory is. End your biography with explaining why Louis Pasteur's work affects what we do today.

(7) Follow up with Herschel's World of Economics as Herschel discusses supply and demand. In the video, how does Herschel's advertisement explain the concept of supply and demand? How are they related? https://www.youtube.com/watch?v=ffwwmHmypek&list=UUFY_hqJBpIJFsyro5Hdk8Vg

(8) Get a few pieces of paper, and prepare yourself to draw the process through which bread is made. Look at all the steps that were listed in this section, and feel free to do any outside research. Number your steps, beginning with the harvesting of wheat and ending with the delivery of bread to stores.

(9) Read the following article about the chicken wing shortage. When you have finished, write three short paragraphs about how the concepts of *Need & Want*, *Supply & Demand*, and *Buyer & Seller* are each related to the rising prices. When you have finished with the three paragraphs, write one additional short one about how everything is connected. http://www.businessweek.com/articles/2013-08-28/why-is-chicken-more-expensive-ask-mcdonalds

(10) We have talked a lot about local trade and production, as well as national, but it also happens on a larger, global scale. The following video from BizKids accurately and entertainingly describes the global economy through interviews and explanations by kids, to help understanding of trade and economy. When you have finished watching the video, write five things that you have learned about the economy, and how each one does or will impact your life.

For Further Reading

Andrews, Carolyn. *What Are Goods and Services?* Crabtree, 2008.

Bauman, Yoram. *The Cartoon Introduction to Economics: Volume One: Microeconomics.* Hill and Wang, 2010.

Bauman, Yoram. *The Cartoon Introduction to Economics: Volume Two: Macroeconomics.* Hill and Wang, 2011.

Challen, Paul. *What is Supply and Demand?* Crabtree, 2010.

Early, Lawrence K. *Kids Economics: Basic Economic and Financial Terms for Kids.* CreateSpace, 2014.

Furgang, Kathy. *National Geographic Kids: Everything Money: A Wealth of Facts, Photos, and Fun!* National Geographic Children's Books, 2013.

Harman, Hollis Page. *Money Sense for Kids.* Barron's Educational Series, 2005.

Larche, Maggie M. *Striker Jones: Elementary Economics for Elementary Detectives.* CreateSpace, 2011.

Larson, Jennifer. *Do I Need It? Or Do I Want It?: Making Budget Choices.* Lerner Classroom, 2010.

Larson, Jennifer. *Who's Buying? Who's Selling?: Understanding Consumers and Producers.* Lerner Classroom, 2010.

Lerner, I.M. *The Secret Under the Staircase.* Under the Staircase: An Economic Adventure Series for Kids, 2013.

Madson, Debbie. *Money Lessons for ids: Teaching Kids About Money.* CreateSpace, 2014.

Maybury, Richard J. *Whatever Happened to Penny Candy: A Fast, Clear, and Fun Explanation of the Economics You Need For Success in Your Career, Business, and Investments.* Bluestocking, 2010.

Orr, Tamra. *A Kid's Guide to the Economy.* Mitchell Lane Publishers, 2009.

Sember, Brette McWhorter. *The Everything Kids' Money Book: Earn it, save it, and watch it grow!* Adams Media, 2008.

Quiz

(1) What is *economy*?
   - (A) How we produce money
   - (B) How we spend money
   - (C) The study how money is exchanged
   - (D) All of the above

(2) Which of the following is NOT a need?
   - (A) A chocolate bar
   - (B) Vegetables
   - (C) Water
   - (D) A house

(3) Which of the following is NOT a want?
   - (A) Pizza
   - (B) Popcorn from the movies
   - (C) Water
   - (D) Lemonade

(4) _____ is the term for what/how much customers want.
   - (A) Supply
   - (B) Demand
   - (C) Want
   - (D) Need

(5) _____ is the term for what you have in stock to sell.
   - (A) Supply
   - (B) Demand
   - (C) Want
   - (D) Need

(6) Which of the following is NOT a good?
   - (A) Getting a haircut
   - (B) Buying a large package of water
   - (C) Purchasing a new car
   - (D) Getting your favorite band's new CD

(7) Which of the following is NOT a service?
   - (A) Getting a haircut
   - (B) Getting your car fixed by a mechanic
   - (C) Getting a pizza on a Friday night
   - (D) Having your hotel room cleaned when you leave

(8) _____ is when you do not rely on others for your needs.
   - (A) Independence
   - (B) Interdependence

(C) Supply

(D) Demand

(9) _____ is when you rely on others for some of your needs.

    (A) Independence

    (B) Interdependence

    (C) Need

    (D) Want

(10) What is the process of making sure that milk is safe for people to drink?

    (A) Sieving

    (B) Pasteurization

    (C) Pastorization

    (D) Interdependence

(11) Why do we use that process for milk?

    (A) Because there are harmful germs in it.

    (B) Because it needs to have a white color, to identify as milk.

    (C) Because mad cow disease is a symptom of drinking unclean milk.

    (D) Because it makes milk more expensive, and gives stores more money.

(12) _____ is using water for your crops.

    (A) Irrigation

    (B) Independence

    (C) Pasteurization

    (D) Demand

(13) Which of the following do farmers use to get water to their crops easily?

    (A) Pasteurization

    (B) Irrigation canals

    (C) Sieving

    (D) Mills

(14) Which of the following concepts describes what goes *in* and *out* of a country?

    (A) Supply and demand

    (B) Want and need

    (C) Import and export

    (D) Independence and interdependence

(15) Which of the following concepts describes what stores *have* and what customers *want*?

    (A) Supply and demand

    (B) Want and need

    (C) Import and export

    (D) Independence and interdependence

(16) If you do not have a lot of money, you should focus on your Needs more than your Wants.

    (A) True

    (B) False

(17) Supply and demand will constantly affect the price of a good.
   (A) True
   (B) False

(18) Irrigation canals were the very first method of watering crops.
   (A) True
   (B) False

(19) You can easily make bread without yeast.
   (A) True
   (B) False

(20) If you are interdependent, you rely on others for needs.
   (A) True
   (B) False

Quiz Answers

(1) **D.** Economy is how we produce, spend, and exchange money.

(2) **A.** A chocolate bar is not a need.

(3) **C.** Water is not a want.

(4) **B.** Demand is the term for what/how much customers want.

(5) **A.** Supply is the term for what you have in stock to sell.

(6) **A.** Getting a haircut is not a good.

(7) **C.** Having a pizza is not a service.

(8) **A.** Independence is when you do not rely on others for needs.

(9) **B.** Interdependence is when you rely on others for your needs.

(10) **B.** Pasteurization is the process of making sure milk is safe for people to drink.

(11) **A.** We use this process because of the harmful germs in unclean milk.

(12) **A.** Irrigation is using water for crops.

(13) **B.** Irrigation canals are used to get water to crops easily.

(14) **C.** Import and export describe what goes in and out of a country.

(15) **A.** Supply and demand describes what stores have and what customers want.

(16) **True.** If you do not have a lot of money, you should focus on Needs more than Wants.

(17) **True.** Supply and demand will constantly affect the price of a good.

(18) **False.** Irrigation canals were not the very first method of watering crops, but were developed later.

(19) **False.** You cannot easily make bread without yeast.

(20) **True.** If you are interdependent, you rely on others for needs.

Section 5: Heroes of America

America's history is short compared to the legendary timelines of Europe, Asia, and Africa. Yet still, students will see that many of history's greatest figures have been born in America and lived to shape our country and the world. Here is a brief overview of America's most successful heroes, and how they affect you today.

Abraham Lincoln

If you ask anyone their favorite American hero, many will likely say Abraham Lincoln. He served as the sixteenth president of the United States, and led the nation during the turbulent period known as the Civil War. During this era, the southern states wanted to secede, or break off and form their own country—but the northern states that this was against the law. The south wanted to preserve *slavery*, their institution of enslaving African-Americans. It was Lincoln's incredible resolve, his intelligence, and his leaderships that helped keep the country together. The northern states eventually conquered the south and stopped them from seceding.

Abraham Lincoln is responsible for ending slavery in America. When the Civil War began in 1861, he did not want to end slavery; in fact, he wanted nothing to do with it. He did not care is the south kept their slaves; he only wanted to keep the United States together, because our constitutions declares that it against the law for a minority to break away from the Union (the United States together). In the north, there was a very small population of people who wanted to *abolish* slavery, which meant they wanted to get rid of it. They were called the *abolitionists*, and at the same they were viewed as completely crazy. Slavery had been around for hundreds of years; you couldn't simply "get rid of it," people said. Until Lincoln came along!

During the course of the war, something changed drastically. Maybe it was the fact that people in the north, through the battles, witnessed the horrible state of slavery in the south. African-Americans were forced to work hours upon hours per day, without pay. They could not escape; they were hurt; they were the property of their white masters.

If you want to understand Abraham Lincoln, an important document to know is the *Emancipation Proclamation*. It was a momentous document issued on January 1, 1863 that essentially declared all slaves in the rebelling states to be free. Of course, the south was embroiled in a war, and the slaveholders, in rebellion, were unwilling to simply give up their slaves. But it inspired many slaves to attempt escape and flee to the north, and it united the northern armies in another common cause: to destroy the completely inhumane system of slavery. This is one of the most important documents in the history of America, aside from the Declaration of Independence and the Constitution. The effect that the Emancipation Proclamation had was incredible; it ended hundreds of years of suffering by African-Americans.

The Civil War ended in 1865, when the south ultimately surrendered to approaching northern armies. But even after the war, many southerners were not happy. On April 14, 1865, just days after a peace treaty had been signed, Abraham Lincoln went to Washington D.C.'s Ford Theatre to see a play. While he was peacefully watching, a man named John Wilkes Booth suddenly appeared behind him. Booth was an actor and had supported the Confederacy (the southern states) throughout the war. Booth, days earlier, had planned to kidnap the president and bring him to the Confederate capital of Richmond, Virginia, but the plan fell through.

Booth wanted to kill Abraham Lincoln and sent the country into chaos. At the same time, counterparts of Booth were executing a plan to assassinate Vice President Andrew Johnson and the Secretary of State, a man named William Seward. In the theatre, Abraham Lincoln was sitting with his wife, and a soldier, Henry Rathbone, and his fiancé. When Booth pulled a gun out and shot Lincoln in the back of his head, Rathbone immediately got up and tried to attack Booth as the theatre dissolved into anarchy. Booth stabbed Rathbone and jumped down onto the stage. He shouted his famous words, "*Sic semper tyrannis!*" This means "Thus ever to tyrants," the motto of the state of Virginia.

Despite the grisly manner of the president's death, he is remembered as, very possibly, our greatest president. He carried us through our bloodiest war and ended slavery, two accomplishments that mark American history to this day.

Jackie Robinson

In the early history of sports, being an African-American athlete was a rarity. Most athletes were white, because of rampant racism in America. Many African-American children grew up knowing how little their chances were of making it big, so many of them decided not to pursue their dreams. But one man, Jackie Robinson, embodied a classic American success story, overcoming racial and physical boundaries on his way to stardom and fame.

He was born in Georgia in 1919 in a single-parent household. Jackie's father was never present in his life, since he left the family around the time that Jackie came into the world. His mother had four other children to take care of, so the Robinson household was almost always struggling. The family moved from Georgia to California, where Jackie was inspired by his siblings, who avidly played sports. One of his brothers, Mack, even went to the Olympics in 1936 for the sport of track.

Jackie Robinson attended the University of California in Los Angeles, where he was a star athlete. He participated in basketball, football, and track, but baseball was always his favorite. There was something about baseball that he loved. Even though he loved baseball, he was going to enter the field of professional football in his post-college years, but there was a major event that stopped him: World War II.

During the war, a *draft* was issued. This meant that people were required to enlist in the army; millions of Americans were shipped to Europe and Asia to fight the enemy countries. Many, however, remained in America for training and would never leave the country.

During World War II, white soldiers and African-American soldiers were not allowed to serve in the same battalion, an example of how racism was alive in America, even almost a hundred years after President Lincoln issued the Emancipation Proclamation. African-Americans were also required to sit in the back of the bus; only whites were allowed in the front. One day, on a bus, Jackie Robinson refused to move to the back of the bus, an action that later made Rosa Parks famous.

He was discharged from the army in 1944, a year before the close of the war. It was then that he turned to baseball to fill his post-army days. He stayed in Kansas and played for the Kansas City Monarchs; at this time, African-Americans were not allowed to play with, or even against, whites. There was a separate "Negro Baseball League."

Negro is what people used to call African-Americans; today, it is a bad word that we do not use.

But times were changing. It was slow, but they were changing. Eventually African-Americans were allowed to play with whites, and Jackie Robinson was immediately brought to Brooklyn, New York to play for a team called the Dodgers. While he was there, he faced tremendous amounts of adversity, from the opposing team and his teammates, as well as the crowd. People hurled threats and bottles at him; sometimes the opposing team boycotted him by not even appearing at the game. But Jackie Robinson, resilient and brave, never let it get to him. He eventually won the MVP Award for his incredible skills.

Why is this important? Jackie Robinson was the first African-American baseball player in major-league baseball. This occurred in the year 1947. Despite all the barriers and records he was breaking, people still hated him, simply because his skin was dark. But he was determined to play the game and change people's minds, and that's exactly what he did. Eventually, people realized that African-Americans could be just as good, and better, than white people at sports. He was a success, and he inspired millions of African-Americans who were also suffering from racism at the time.

Jackie Robinson was added to the Baseball Hall of Fame, and you can even watch a movie made about him, called *42* (his baseball number). He died in 1972, but his legacy still lives on.

Martin Luther King, Jr.

Abraham Lincoln may have abolished slavery in the midst of the Civil War in the 1860s, but that does not mean that African-Americans suddenly gained equality or that racism was put to an end. In fact, harsh racism continued for over a century after the Emancipation Proclamation, and there is still evidence of racism in our society. One man who ardently fought against racism and for equality was Martin Luther King, Jr., named after his father. We'll call him MLK for convenience!

Throughout the 1950s and the 1960s, the Civil Rights movement picked up steam, fighting for African-American quality. During this time, many areas were *segregated*, which means that there were water fountains for whites, and water fountain for colored people; whites sat in the front of the bus, while colored people sat in the back. There were schools for whites, and schools for African-Americans; restrooms for whites, restrooms for African-Americans. Sure, slavery was no longer institutionalized in America, but the racist divide made African-Americans suffer still.

MLK worked in churches and gave people hope. He knew that using violence was no way to achieve peace. He believed the peace could only be achieved through peace, not fighting; so he advocated non-violent ways of getting what they want. One of the most successful endeavors was called the *Montgomery Bus Boycott*, which started in Montgomery, Alabama. African-Americans suddenly refused to ride the bus to work and school each day, in order to deprive the bus companies of payment. If the buses would be segregated, then African-Americans would walk to work. Suddenly, thousands of people joined in and walked together in crowds in the morning and evening. Eventually, bus segregation was forced to an end because the bus companies were losing so much money.

Many people saw MLK as a threat, however, including the police. Peaceful protests for equality incited angry riots by white people that wanted to keep segregation; they would attack the peaceful protestors. Police would even attack the peaceful protestors, using high-power hoses to blast water at them until they ran away, or even arresting him. MLK was unjustly arrested on more than one occasion and released.

In 1963, a hundred years after Lincoln's Emancipation Proclamation, MLK delivered one of the most momentous speeches in American history. It was called the "I Have a Dream," and you may have even heard that line before. In Washington D.C., the United States capital, MLK delivered the speech to over 250,000 eager listeners. In his speech, he declared that white and colored people cannot work separately; if we want to achieve equality, we need to put aside our differences and make sure society is a better place, especially for our children.

The very next year, the Civil Rights Act was passed by President Lyndon B. Johnson. Slowly, step-by-step, King's dream was becoming a reality.

He had a lot of supporters, but he also had a lot of enemies. One of them was a man named James Earl, who could stand the thought of white and colored people living peacefully together. He killed Martin Luther King, Jr. on April 4th, 1968, which set off riots across the country. People were upset by his death, because they viewed it as a setback; but they knew they needed to keep on fighting for equality. Just like many heroic Americans who met untimely deaths, King's legacy still lives on today, and we celebrate his birthday every year, on the third Monday of January.

Helen Keller

It's tough to study heroic Americans without mentioning the name of Helen Keller. No, she was not involved in politics or war or sports, but she inspired millions of people across the globe. She was an American woman, both blind and deaf, who eventually learned to read, write, and even talk. She was born in Alabama in 1880; her parents were happy to have a joyful and happy baby around the house. But something happened after she turned one year old; she came down with a terrible fever and, the doctors thought, a headache. After this sickness, she was never the same. Her parents and the doctors discovered that the baby Helen no longer could see, or even hear. In the matter of a few days, Helen had lost her vision and her hearing.

As you can imagine, it is almost impossible to get around without vision and hearing. In order to communicate with people, she had to move her hands or make grunting noises. She easily became angry because of how irritating this way of living was; she could see what her parents looked like; she could not talk to them, or even hear their voices. It was a horrible way to grow up.

When Helen Keller was seven years old, her parents hired a specialist to come and see her. The specialist's name was Annie Sullivan, and she had been blind before she had surgery on her eyes, which allowed her to see again. She worked in Boston, at the Perkins Institute for the Blind, and immediately came down to Alabama to help Helen.

You are probably wondering how Helen Keller learned anything – how did she learn to read? How did she know what words were? Annie Sullivan would put something into her hand: a book, for example. Once Helen had felt the book, Annie would press small letters onto Helen's hand, spelling the word B-O-O-K for her. Helen began to get the idea and to identify objects. Once she knew words, she could then learn braille. *Braille* is just like the alphabet, except each letter is a number of dots in a certain shape, that a blind person can feel and recognize. Once Helen Keller knew braille, she could read anything!

But now you're probably wondering how she learned to speak! She had another teacher, one named Sarah Fuller. She would place her hand on Sarah Fuller's lips, and feel the words that she was saying. She started small, just speaking basic words, which then evolved into phrases, and then into whole sentences! At this point, there was nothing stopping Helen Keller from attending college; she was immediately accepted to a Massachusetts school called Radcliffe College.

At school, Annie Sullivan went pretty much everywhere Helen went, including class! Helen would listen to the lectures from her professors, and then press the words into her hand. While in school, she wrote a number of articles about her life and what her condition was like; these were eventually strung together and published under the title *The Story of My Life*. In 1936, she was granted the Theodore Roosevelt Distinguished Service Medal for all of her hard work.

Later in life, Helen Keller worked mainly with other blind people, helping them find inspiration and home in their everyday life. She toured the United States, gave speeches, answered questions, and showed the world that, no matter how tough the obstacle is, you can overcome in. She lived during the World War II era, when many American soldiers returned to their country injured and hurt. She would often spend time with them and encourage them to keep fighting, keep going, and never give up. She also spent a lot of time raising money to help educate blind people; many blind people attend schools just for them, and at this point in American history, many of them were severely underfunded.

Throughout her life, she became famous, meeting people like Mark Twain, a popular classic author; Alexander Graham Bell, the inventor of the telephone; and all of the United States presidents between Grover Cleveland and Lyndon Johnson: Presidents William McKinley, Theodore Roosevelt, William Taft, Woodrow Wilson, Warren Harding, Calvin Coolidge, Herbert Hoover, Franklin Delano Roosevelt, Harry Truman, Dwight Eisenhower, and John F. Kennedy. That's a lot of presidents!

There was a television show made about her life, which premiered in 1957. It was called *The Miracle Worker*, and the producers used a lot of material from *The Story of My Life*, her book, to make the show.

In 1961, Helen Keller wasn't feeling that well. She was eighty years old now, and she had definitely made her mark upon the world. Just three years later, she would receive the Presidential Medal of Freedom, and the year after that, she would be elected into the Women's Hall of Fame, all for her outstanding achievements and bravery during her lifetime.

In 1968, Helen Keller unfortunately passed away. It was not a rough death, but an easy one. She simply passed away in her sleep; if she had to die, this was the probably the simplest way. Today, her memory still inspires people who are born with disabilities. Looking at how much Helen Keller did, before so much adversity, it gives a lot of people hope.

These American heroes all have something in common: They faced *a lot* of challenges, but through dedication and hard work, they succeeded in the end. Helen Keller was faced with the inability to speak or walk, but she learned to do those things despite all odds. Martin Luther King Jr. managed to unite millions of people against blatant racism, just as Jackie Robinson showed the world what he could do, inspiring African-Americans everywhere. Abraham Lincoln rescued a nation that was being torn in half and gave freedom to millions of slaves, forever changing the face of America. Through studying these four American heroes, we can get a better image of American history, and what it means to be a hero. Next time you face a challenge in your life, just think back to these amazing American heroes, and hopefully you will be inspired to overcome the challenge, no matter how much you might feel down!

Discussion Questions

(1) How would history have been different if Abraham Lincoln had not signed the Emancipation Proclamation? Do you think slaves would have been eventually freed by another president? Why or why not?

(2) Out of all the heroes here, which one is the *most* heroic? Or are they all the same?

(3) Do you watch sports? How do you think sports would be different if there were not any African-American players?

(4) Why do you think it took so long for African-Americans to finally get civil rights in the 1960s, when they were freed from slavery in the 1860s? Why the hundred-year gap?

(5) Do you think Helen Keller would have learned to speak and talk without help from her teacher, Annie Sullivan?

(6) Think about one hero that was not in this section. It can be someone from history, someone from a story, or one of your friends/family members. What makes them heroic? Remember this for the Activities section.

(7) Abraham Lincoln used the expression "A house divided against itself cannot stand," which immediately became a famous string of words. When you think about his presidency, what does this expression mean? If you keep up with current events in America, does the phrase still have meaning today? How can you use it in your life?

(8) What made Helen Keller a hero? She was not involved in sports, like Jackie Robinson, or in politics, like Lincoln and MLK. Who did Helen Keller affect, and how did this change them?

(9) Why do you think sports was such an important field to change? In other words, what long-lasting changes did Jackie Robinson have on the United States?

(10) Both Jackie Robinson and MLK helped revolutionize African-American rights. What place does African-American history have in the history of the United States?

Activities

(1) For each of the heroes in this section, create a timeline that lasts from their birth until their death. You may have to do some additional research on the Internet or in the library; make sure to list all the significant events in their lives.

(2) Watch the following video about Abraham Lincoln and his successes during the Civil War. At the end, list *three* interesting facts about him! https://www.youtube.com/watch?v=MFABcUUJMrl

(3) The "dream" that MLK had was one of equality and a better world. Write about a dream that you have: what do you hope for? How would you like to change the world for the better? Write a page on this subject, and make sure to be creative and go into detail! Give us the vision of a world in which your dream is reality.

(4) Watch the following educational cartoon on Helen Keller. In this section, we talked about Helen Keller as a hero, but when you watch this video, think about Annie Sullivan, her teacher. Do you think that Annie was a hero too? The video discusses the virtue of patience. How did patience help Annie? Did Annie have any other traits that helped her help Helen? https://www.youtube.com/watch?v=1tKG2j03wGM

(5) Pick someone that you think is a hero. It can be someone from history, someone from a book, a show, one of your friends, or a family member. Draw of picture of him or her, and then write a paragraph or two about why you think they are a hero. What did they do that makes them special? How do they affect the people around them?

(6) Now that you have read about the "I Have a Dream" speech, watch it here! After watching it, write down a few reasons that explain why MLK is a great orator (someone who gives speeches). What does he say that gets people excited? Write down if you think this is a good speech or not. https://www.youtube.com/watch?v=vx3Z8ZToq3c

(7) Both Abraham Lincoln and Martin Luther King, Jr. were assassinated by people who did not like what they were doing. Research the assassins, and create a single biography page about each. Focus on motivations. *Why* did they do what they did? What was the purpose? Why did they disagree with Lincoln and King?

(8) The following movie clip features a scene from the film *42*, about Jackie Robinson, as Jackie and his friend Pee Wee take the field during a game. After watching it, answer the following questions: https://www.youtube.com/watch?v=vx3Z8ZToq3c
   (a) Why did the crowd start booing when Pee Wee put his arm across Jackie?
   (b) What does Pee Wee mean when he says he needs his family "to know who I am?"

(9) Helen Keller often communicated through the use of Braille. Take a look at this website that teaches you the Braille alphabet; feel free to explore the website and even learn the alphabet. This will give you a basic idea of the system of communication that she used. http://braillebug.afb.org/Games.asp

(10) Pick one of the four heroes that we discussed in this section. You are going to create your own biography of them. Take three pieces of plain paper, and fold them in half (hamburger-style). It should now look like a small book. Make sure to include a cover. If you'd like, you can reference your timeline from Activity One to give you all the significant events in your like. Pictures are also a great way to illustrate their lives!

For Further Reading

Adler, David A. *A Picture Book of Helen Keller.* Holiday House, 1992.

Bader, Bonnie. *Who Was Martin Luther King, Jr?* Penguin Young Readers Group, 2007.

Davis, Burke. *Black Heroes of the American Revolution.* Houghton Mifflin Harcourt, 1992.

Denenberg, Dennis. *50 American Heroes Every Kid Should Meet!* Lerner Publishing Group, 2005.

Editors of TIME for Kids. *Jackie Robinson: Strong Inside and Out.* HarperCollins, 2005.

Harweck, Dona. *Martin Luther King, Jr.* Teacher Created Materials, 2011.

Herbert, Janis. *Abraham Lincoln for Kids: His Life and Times with 21 Activities.* Chicago Review Press, 2007.

Herman, Gail. *Who Was Jackie Robinson?* Grosset & Dunlap, 2010.

Hurwitz, Johanna. *Helen Keller: Courage in the Dark.* Random House, 1997.

Meltzer, Brad. *I Am Abraham Lincoln.* Dial, 2014.

O'Connor, Jim. *Jackie Robinson and the Story of All Black Baseball.* Random House, 1989.

Pascal, Janet. *Who Was Abraham Lincoln?* Penguin Young Readers Group, 2008.

Petruccio, Steven James. *American Heroes Coloring Book.* Dover Publications, 2013.

Schott, Jane A. *How Did Martin Luther King, Jr. Make History?* Sterling, 2014.

Thompson, Gare. *Who Was Helen Keller?* Grosset & Dunlap, 2003.

Quiz

(1) What position did Abraham Lincoln hold in the United States government?
   (A) Secretary of State
   (B) Army general
   (C) President
   (D) Vice-president

(2) During what war did Abraham Lincoln serve in this position?
   (A) American Revolution
   (B) War of 1812
   (C) Civil War
   (D) World War II

(3) What document declared that all slaves were now free?
   (A) The "I Have a Dream" speech
   (B) The Emancipation Proclamation
   (C) The 15th Amendment
   (D) The Constitution

(4) What sport is Jackie Robinson known for?
   (A) Baseball
   (B) Basketball
   (C) Track
   (D) Swimming

(5) During what war was Jackie Robinson drafted into the army?
   (A) The Civil War
   (B) World War I
   (C) World War II
   (D) The Korean War

(6) Why was Jackie Robinson discharged from the army?
   (A) He was colorblind
   (B) He refused to move to the back of a bus
   (C) He demanded to fight with white soldiers
   (D) He was playing baseball after-hours

(7) What method did Martin Luther King say was most effective in achieving his goals?
   (A) Violent fighting
   (B) Peaceful protest
   (C) Going to church every Sunday
   (D) Nothing; he did not think they had a chance at success

(8) What speech is MLK known for?
   (A) The Emancipation Proclamation
   (B) "I Have a Dream"

(C) "I Wish for Freedom"
(D) "And We'll Never Be Royals"

(9) What movement did MLK fight for?
   (A) The Civil Rights movement
   (B) The Chinese Inclusion movement
   (C) The Gender Equality movement
   (D) The Student Rights movement

(10) What was the name of Helen Keller's teacher?
   (A) Annie Sullivan
   (B) Marie Curie
   (C) Jackie Robinson
   (D) Sarah J. Parker

(11) What is the name of the alphabet that Helen Keller learned to read?
   (A) Morse code
   (B) Roman alphabet
   (C) Greek alphabet
   (D) Braille alphabet

(12) Which of the following did Helen Keller NOT learn how to do?
   (A) Read
   (B) Write
   (C) Speak
   (D) None of the above; she learned all of them!

(13) Who said the following quote: "A house divided against itself cannot stand."
   (A) Abraham Lincoln
   (B) Jackie Robinson
   (C) Martin Luther King, Jr.
   (D) Helen Keller

(14) Who said the following quote: "I have a dream."
   (A) Abraham Lincoln
   (B) Jackie Robinson
   (C) Martin Luther King, Jr.
   (D) Helen Keller

(15) What was the Montgomery Bus Boycott?
   (A) An event in which thousands of African-American workers refused to build more buses for the city of Montgomery, Alabama
   (B) An event in which thousands of African-American students and professors only took buses around the city; they refused to walk or take cabs
   (C) An event in which thousands of white people refused to ride buses, because African-Americans were allowed to use them
   (D) An event in which thousands of African-Americans refused to ride buses, because they were forced to sit in the back

(16) Helen Keller was born blind and deaf.
    (A) True
    (B) False

(17) Abraham Lincoln wanted the southern states to secede so that America could become two countries.
    (A) True
    (B) False

(18) Jackie Robinson was the first African-American baseball player in the major leagues.
    (A) True
    (B) False

(19) Martin Luther King, Jr. said that using violent protest methods were okay.
    (A) True
    (B) False

(20) Despite learning how to read, Helen Keller never learned how to write.
    (A) True
    (B) False

Quiz Answers

(1) **C.** Abraham Lincoln was the president of the United States.

(2) **C.** Abraham Lincoln served as president during the Civil War.

(3) **B.** The Emancipation Proclamation declared that the slaves were free.

(4) **A.** Jackie Robinson is known for baseball.

(5) **C.** Jackie Robinson was drafted into the army during World War II.

(6) **B.** Jackie Robinson was discharged because he refused to move to the back of a bus.

(7) **B.** MLK said that peaceful protest was most effective in achieving his goals.

(8) **B.** MLK is most known for his "I Have a Dream" speech.

(9) **A.** MLK fought for the Civil Rights movement.

(10) **A.** Helen Keller's teacher was Annie Sullivan.

(11) **D.** Helen Keller learned the Braille alphabet.

(12) **D.** Helen Keller learned to read, write, and speak.

(13) **A.** Abraham Lincoln said "A house divided against itself cannot stand."

(14) **C.** MLK said "I have a dream."

(15) **D.** The Montgomery Bus Boycott was an event in which thousands of African-Americans refused to ride buses, because they were forced to sit in the back.

(16) **False.** Helen Keller was born with her sight and hearing.

(17) **False.** Abraham Lincoln wanted the north and south to stay together.

(18) **True.** Jackie Robinson was the first African-American baseball player in the major leagues.

(19) **False.** MLK did not think that violent protest methods were okay.

(20) **False.** Helen Keller did learn how to write.

CPSIA information can be obtained
at www.ICGtesting.com
Printed in the USA
LVHW061509071020
668213LV00007B/487